Internet Dating Secrets Revealed!

Learn how to meet and attract amazing women using the internet!

By Sam Stone

© 2006 – 2007 all rights reserved

Legal Notice!

This book is copyright 2006 - 2007 with all rights reserved. It is illegal to copy, distribute, and/or create derivative works from this book in whole or in part or to contribute to the copying, distribution, or creating of derivative works of this book. By taking possession of this book, you agreed to the statement similar to this one that was listed on the website where the book was purchased from:

"©2006 - 2007, All Rights Reserved. All content included in this book, is the property of Thundercorp International Development LLC Do not try to or copy, steal, or distribute all or any part of this book or this web site without written permission. If you do so, I will have my team of attorneys make you wish that you'd never done so.

By reading this book, you agree to the following: You understand that the information contained on this page and in this book is an opinion, and it should be used for personal entertainment purposes only. You are responsible for your own behavior, and this book or any part of it is not to be considered legal, professional or personal advice. You also agree that Thundercorp International Development LLC. or/and any of its employees, managers or/and shareholders will not be responsible for any loss you suffer as a result of reading this book or acting on the information within."

If you did happen to "find" this book on the internet/borrowed it from a friend/got it in email from an anonymous benefactor, I hope you realize that I put a lot of effort into this and I'm sure you've gained a lot of value from this book so please find it in your heart to do the right thing and purchase a legal copy of it.

Visit www.onlinedatingpro.com for more information on this title.
ISBN: 978-0-6151-5956-0

Introduction

It was a cold and stormy Saturday night...

Ok, it was actually quite nice, but it was a Saturday night, and I was sitting all alone in my apartment wondering how to get started.

I was new in town, didn't have any friends, and didn't even know where to find a good social scene. So I decided to try out this thing I heard about called "online dating". I put up a profile on match.com and waited for the stream of emails from beautiful women to flood my inbox, but alas, there were none.

Being the "go getter" that I am, I decided to be proactive and search for the girl of my dreams. I found several profiles with pictures of women that seemed nice and attractive, and sent out several long emails telling them all about myself and my personality.

Still, no response... I was ready to call it quits, but then decided that it can't be THAT complicated to meet women online and that I can and will figure out this whole online dating thing and get really good at it!

Now I'm not ugly or anything, but I definitely don't have the tall-dark-handsome-look, and I'm not rich or famous, yet during that year, I've met countless women, and received thousands of emails (literally – thousands!). I've had several meaningful relationships with a few amazing women, and met some of my best female friends through online dating. There were weeks that all I did was go out with women I met online, sometimes 9 or 10 dates a week – not that I'm complaining or anything – but that was really hard!!!

In the process, I've also been burnt a few times, had some very disappointing experiences, and learned a lot from them. These experiences have lead to develop the "Sam Stone™ method"

Currently, I'm in a 8 month relationship with a very special woman that I met on one of the dating sites I tried out.

My friends (both male and female) heard of my success, and started asking me for advice. Over time I put together a list of tips and ideas that would help them navigate the complexities of online dating and go from no success at all, to several dates a week, to getting into relationships and going from total disappointment from the lack of compatible dates, to having to get advice on time management because of the multitude of new women they are meeting. At some point, they said, "you should write a book on this" and so I did.

What will the Sam Stone™ method do for you?

If you read this book, follow the step by step guide that I describe and apply the concepts I talk about, you will find that your life is no longer as it used to be. You will go from very little or no success with women to having more dates then you can handle every week. You will be so swamped with women, that you will find yourself turning down women that just a short time ago you could only dream of having. This system is not unique to me! Others who have used this method are seeing the same results!

Whether you are an experienced "online dater" looking to increase your success, or a novice looking for a guide to this new world on online dating, this book will help you find the answers that you are looking for.

This book is not meant to be used as a novel. It is a reference manual for online dating. The best way to use it is to read it cover to cover at least twice and find the parts that apply to you. Take note all of the ideas, skills, and techniques and templates that you would like to use to improve your online success.

This book has been written by observing both males and females and how they "operate" online. I've experienced and tested these ideas first hand, so I feel very comfortable giving this advice. It was very important for me to be able to provide advice from a woman's perspective as well, so I conducted many interviews with women who have experience with online dating, and got some very valuable advice from them. I've also spent hours (!) watching how women use online dating, and how they react to different kinds of profiles, emails and sites, and adjusted my method accordingly.

I've included some very helpful exercises that will make this whole process much easier (bet you didn't think there would be homework in this book... ;) I highly recommend that you actually take the time to do them and not just read through them.

For those of you who are thinking that all I teach here is "dirty tricks to get guys laid" or that "I have to lie and not be myself" I would say that this isn't the case. What I teach here is a method that allows you to distill and exhibit your best self (the best qualities you already have) and give a woman the experience of a life time without having to work too hard or spend too much money.

That was my approach to meeting women, sure, I could get laid more if I was a total asshole, but I preferred to get thank you notes from women I took on dates, or even had short relationships with (I actually had women that I broke up with send me thank you cards (!) for the wonderful experience they had with me...). Good karma is better then bad karma...

One last thing:

This book is not intended to be a "silver bullet" that will turn you to an online dating guru over night. The ideas in this book take some practice, and you will eventually have to apply them to your own style and personality. I am asking you to make a commitment to try these ideas out for 90 days. You will notice a significant improvement in your success rate with online dating, but you will have to be persistent and not give up at the first sign of trouble.

It's a bit like learning to walk. You fall down a lot at the beginning, but if you'd have quit then, you'd still be crawling around from place to place. I think that's not the ideal mode of travel.

So sit back, relax, and let the fun begin...

Table of contents:

Introduction to the Sam Stone™ method 8

Part One: Attitude

The online dating mindset

    Chapter 1: **What do you want?** 11

    Chapter 2: **The ideal relationship** 14

    Chapter 3: **Who are you?** 16

    Chapter 4: **Tying it all together** 19

Part Two: Profile

How to create a great profile

    Chapter 5: **Online dating services and how to use them** 22

    Chapter 6: **The "About Me" section** 26

    Chapter 7: **The "What am I looking for" section** 33

    Chapter 8: **The Picture** 35

    Chapter 9: **Profile miscellaneous and advanced technique** 41

Part Three: Locate and IM/eMail

Find and communicate with the girl of your dreams

    Chapter 10: **The Search** 47

    Chapter 11: **Communication** 53

    Chapter 12: **What do I say?** 57

    Chapter 13: **The email exchange** 67

    Chapter 14: **The Sam Stone™ email method** 71

Part Four: The date

The Sam Stone™ date method.

    Chapter 15: **Part 1 - Setup and mindset** 89

    Chapter 16: **Part 2 - The introduction and early part of the date** 94

    Chapter 17: **Part 3 – Mid-date** 104

    Chapter 18: **Part 4 – Ending the date – kiss and future plans** 117

    Chapter 19: **Epilogue** 128

    Appendix A: **Friendship with women** 130

    Appendix B: **Your personal "video game" success plan** 132

The Sam Stone™ Method

Over the past few years, I've been very active with online dating, and through lots of trial and error, and a lot of observation and discussion with the women I met, I've found that there are some patterns that keep recurring in most situations. These patters can be isolated, analyzed and most importantly, replicated and learned.

The Sam Stone™ method is the culmination of these learnings. This method, is a framework that you can apply to yourself and your personality. You will have to do some work, but the results you get will be worth it. The Sam Stone™ method will allow you to create your own material and stories and will allow you to present an "authentic you" that is attractive and desirable to the women you meet online.

I've come up with this acronym (pronounces "applied")

APL-IED
Attitude - Profile - Locate – IM/eMail – Date

Attitude:
The first step in the Sam Stone™ method, is to align your inner self to the proper attitude for online dating. This is an environment that will be new to you at first. You will face challenges, and even disappointment, before you reach true success. My goal is to help minimize those initial hardships and make the process as smooth as possible for you.

Profile:
Your profile is your first vehicle to convey your personality and attract women. I will be teaching you how to optimize your profile,

and how you can present your best self to attract women online no matter what you look like/how much money you make/you job, etc...

Locate:

In this step of the process I will teach you how to find the type of women you are looking for. I will also teach you some strategies that will allow you to maximize your time and prevent you from wasting your time on women you will either never meet or that are not the ones you want to meet.

IM/eMail:

This is one of the most important parts in meeting women online. The Sam Stone™ method will provide you with extensive information, samples and advice on how to write great emails that will make you attractive and how to get to meet a girl without even having to get her phone number. I will also teach you how to get a woman to go out with you with an exchange of only 3 emails.

Date:

This is really not online dating anymore, you are now in the real world, but this is important if you want to create a relationship (short or long term). I will teach you how to structure your first date to ensure that the first date is not the last.

Part 1: Attitude: The online dating mindset

In this section, I am going to teach you how to approach online dating and how to create a plan to save yourself from making mistakes that could ruin your online dating experience.

- Give me six hours to chop down a tree and I will spend the first four sharpening the axe.

Abraham Lincoln

Chapter 1: What do you want?

I've seem many people go into online dating without any idea of what they are looking for. It's kinda funny actually.

Imagine buying a new car.

You have a general idea of the type of car you want, but do you go into a dealership and say "hey, I want a nice car, show me what you've got"? Of course not! Most people do at least some research, deciding on a certain body type, and price range. Sometimes color, make and model are a factor, sometimes fuel economy, sometimes features (by the way, if you don't do any of the above, I have this great 1980 dodge station wagon for sale, it's only $50,000... give me a call...;)

So why approach online dating differently? Whether you are looking for the love of your life, a short term relationship, or just to meet some fun new friends, you've got to go into this with at least some idea of where you are going.

Exercise 1

Step 1:

Take a piece of paper, and write down all the qualities you've found attractive in your significant other in previous relationships or that you think you would like to have in a good relationship. Don't hold back. Write everything and anything that comes to mind. Be it physical qualities, personality, social and financial qualities, age, physical location, religion, values, lifestyle, etc...

A great way I found to make this work is to close your eyes (you might want to finish reading this paragraph first... ;), and imagine the feelings you've had in the best moments of your past relationships, what is the situation you are in? what behaviors are happening during

---

this time? What kind of qualities are you looking at in your partner while these great feelings are taking place?

Step 2:
Now take that list and pick the top 15 qualities that you consider important. If you don't have 15 qualities in your list, you might want to repeat step 1 again.

Step 3:
Once again, look at those 15 qualities, and narrow them down to the top 5 most important.

Step 4:
Now you have 3 lists, the key qualities that you can't live without (top 5), the important qualities that you feel should be in your future date, and some (hopefully many) qualities that would be "nice to haves"

Step 5:
Read those lists again, you will need to be comfortable with them because they will be the basis of your future searches. If you don't feel comfortable with any of the qualities on the list, then change them until you are. This list will also change with time, it's not etched in stone.

Step 6:
Now repeat step 1-5 but this time think of all the bad qualities you've experienced in past relationships. Again, don't hold back, write down anything and everything that comes to mind and narrow the list down to the top 15 and the top 5.

Step 7:
Now you have a list of the "deal breakers" these are the qualities that you can't live with and have troubled you in past relationships. Keep

that list in mind when you start looking at the different profiles. You might want to email that hottie who's profile you've just read - who cares if she is a recovering alcoholic with a manic depressive personality who enjoys long walks on the beach and torturing small animals for fun... ;)

I'm exaggerating of course, but there will be a time where you think that you can live with someone who possess a "deal breaker" quality, but that will eventually come back to haunt you if the relationship develops in the future. It's much easier to avoid the problem in an early stage then have to deal with it when you already are in a relationship.

Chapter 2: The ideal relationship

My approach to online dating was to provide a positive experience for both myself and the women I will be meeting. Of course, there is a lot of dishonesty out there (more on that in the next sections), but I feel that if you start your relationship with dishonesty, it will only end up causing pain to the other person, and that's something that ideally shouldn't happen.

Think about the relationship you are looking for. Online dating can be a great way to meet people for all types of relationships:

You could be looking for the wife of your dreams, a long term relationship or perhaps you are just looking for a fun time with no strings attached. You might even be trying to make new friends with the possibility of future romance.

In any case, you need to be true to yourself and know what you are looking for.

There will be times that you will be tempted to contact someone who is not looking for a similar type of relationship, this could lead to lots of disappointment and heartache in the future so you might as well figure out what you want now, rather then try to change someone else in the future.

That said, the answer to this question doesn't have to be a single choice, you could find out you are looking for some uncommitted fun with a possibility for future commitment but you do need to decide that that is what you want and keep that in mind while searching.

By now, you should have a clear idea of what you are looking for. This is great because this will facilitate your search process. Before we get into the nitty-gritty of things there is one more thing you need to do.

Chapter 3: Who are you?

I've seen so many profiles opening with the sentence "it's hard to describe myself..."

Yes, it is hard, but describing yourself in an appealing way is one of the keys to online dating success. A great person with a bad description will have a hard time succeeding and an average person with a great profile will be able to get much further in the online dating process then he could in real life.

So who are you? What's important to you as a person? What can you provide to a relationship? What makes you special?

Exercise 2

Step 1:
On a piece of paper, start writing down the things that are important to you in life, it could be your values, it could be your possessions, it could be family, also think about hobbies and interests you have, just write down anything that comes to mind. You might want to do this part of the exercise on 2 different days, sometimes it helps to "sleep on it" to get a complete list.
Think about your life, what are the interesting things in your life that you feel you would like to share with a partner?

Step 2:
You should have a significant list of qualities, values, and interests (I would try to get at least 50). Read through the list, the items on the list should start to group themselves into different categories (e.g. hobbies, art, spiritual needs, etc...). Feel free to edit the list and tweak it so that you can clearly see the areas of life that you feel are more important to you then others.

> e.g.: I am a vegetarian, and when I wrote my list, I found that I had several items that relate to animals and to nature and the environment. This was very helpful to know, because it explained the feeling I had every time I saw a picture of a girl in a hunting outfit with a gun in her hand (I live in TX...), or one with the huge fish she just caught. I knew that even though she has some great qualities, that relationship will most likely not work in the long run.

Actually I had an ulterior motive for this exercise... I want you to look at the list you have – you have about 50 or more items that make you special. I don't want to sound too sappy or "new age" but you are a special individual, you have a lot to offer to a relationship (now if your list is fully made up of things like sitting home alone all day and playing with your computer and watching TV all day you might want to go out and get some more interesting hobbies...;) you are the reward in this whole game and women should be happy to get the chance to meet you!
Remember – you are the reward!

Detachment:

Now, read this next part carefully! If there is one thing I want you to remember from this book, it's this next thing – I don't care if you fall out of a plane, land on your head and suffer from amnesia – you will remember this! I'm talking about **detachment**.

<u>**Detachment** from results</u> is one of the most important things you can do when learning a new skill. This applies to learning skills with women as well. At least for a while, until you get really good at this, you will need to imagine that you are playing a "video game". This game's goal is to get through different levels and do it consistently. E.g. The first level's goal is to get a response or multiple responses to emails you set up by setting up a good profile. You will

play this game until you can easily and consistently get responses to your first emails.

Like in every video game, you will fail at first, and it might take you a while to get good at it. Do you break down and get emotional when something bad happens to you in a video game? No (if you do, then you need some help...) you just hit restart and play it again. Hopefully, you also learn from your mistake and try not to do it again. It's the same with online dating. You will get ignored, you will get shot down, you will get girls who will call you an asshole, and you will have girls try to mess with you. You will even have girls flake out on you and not show up to dates (once you get good at this, this will happen very infrequently, but it does happen). If you attach yourself to the results, and let them effect your emotions and how you play this "game" then you will lose, because you are giving away the power you have and letting someone else (that you don't even know yet) control it. Sometimes it will hurt, like when you think things are going well, and suddenly a girl stops communicating with you, but you've gotta get back to the game, and play another round.

Detachment from results is the best way to get really good at this, you are the reward, this is a game, you just play it, win or lose, doesn't matter, you are just playing a game. Whatever your goal will be, you will achieve it much faster and with less pain if you see each failure as a learning opportunity and not as an indicator of your character or a quality in your life. **REMEMBER! *DETACHMENT*** If you have to print it out and stick it on your bathroom mirror, or read it out loud to yourself every day, then do it. **This is really important!**

See appendix B for your customizable personal game plan to achieve this!

Chapter 4: Tying it all together

Now that you know who you are, what you are looking for in a partner, what you're NOT looking for in a partner, and what type of relationship you are looking for, you are ready to get into the mix of things and start creating your profile.

One last thing:
I'm sure you'd like to meet someone interesting and fun, but if all you do during the week is spend time at work and all your time on weekends playing video games by yourself (see the movie "40 year old virgin" as an example) then you will have lots of trouble finding someone like that. It's important that you get a life, meet some interesting people, have some hobbies, and create a well rounded personality. You could join a gym and take some classes, find a local university and look at continued education for adults, volunteer at your favorite charity, etc. just be creative and you'll find that not only will you have a lot more to say about yourself, you will also start to enjoy more of your life.

Summary:

In this section we talked about the initial planning that needs to take place in order to make the online dating experience a success. We talked about:
Finding out what are the qualities you are looking for in a person
What "deal breakers" you should keep in mind when searching through profiles and figuring out what type of relationship you are looking for. Finally, we talked about figuring out what are the qualities that you possess that will have an impact on your dating life, and the attitude you will need to succeed.

In the next section, we'll be discussing the profile, the various online services that are out there and how to optimize your profile for the more popular ones, thoughts on what types of photo to use, and how to make your profile stand out from the thousands of profiles on these sites and attract the right kind of attention.

We will also be talking about white lies, and when it is appropriate to use them on a profile.

We'll end part 2 with some cool techniques that will teach you how to leap straight past your "competition" and make a great connection with the people you are interested in.

See you in part 2...

Part Two: The Profile

In this section you will learn all about setting up a profile on the leading dating services, how to make your profile more attractive and alluring, how to make your profile attract the right kind of attention, and how to use photos to your advantage and make yourself shine.

"Do but take care to express yourself in a plain, easy Manner, in well-chosen, significant and decent Terms, and to give a harmonious and pleasing Turn to your Periods: study to explain your Thoughts, and set them in the truest Light, laboring as much as possible, not to leave them dark nor intricate, but clear and intelligible."

-Miguel de Cervantes, Preface to Don Quixote

Chapter 5: Online dating services and how to use them.

There are many online dating sites out there, ranging from national and even global sites like match.com to neighborhood dating sites. There are also sites for specific religions, nationalities and races, and other types of groups.

I can't say I've seen them all, or tried them all, but I have tried out some of the major ones and this is what I've found:

match.com: (let's call this type of site the "generic profile" type)

My personal favorite is match.com. I believe it is one of the most popular sites out there these days.
What I like about match: match is very easy to use, it has a very versatile search engine that allows you to customize your search. You can also save your searches and go back to them and customize them even more if you are looking for something specific or if you want to expand your search a bit.

Match.com allows you to apply different kinds of sorting options and filters to your search results, have specific categories in the profile which makes it easier to read and to write, and also suggest "similar profiles" to the ones you've selected which are sometimes missed by the search.

Match also offers subscribers the ability to view the people who checked their profile out. If there is someone who you like on that list, you could take the initiative and email them in case they are too shy.

What I didn't like about match: match has a superficial aspect to it. Most people I know usually browse by photo, and don't even read a profile if the photo isn't appealing at first glance (although there are ways to get around that as you will see late in this book). It is also a bit less private because you don't even have to be a member to see who's on there (someone I know found out that her office mate is gay by searching that section on match. Needless to say that her friend was not yet ready to "be outed" at the office and the whole scene was very embarrassing for all).

eHarmony/Chemistry.com:

eHarmony has an interesting spin on dating sites. Their thing is personality matching. Since I'm really into personality tests I immediately liked the idea that I'd be matched with people that match my personality. I was surprise at how accurate it is sometimes, most of my better relationships were from eHarmony and I've met some great friends there too.

What I liked about eHarmony: obviously the personality matching is far superior to any other system I've seen out there; it also provides you with a great deal of privacy by not letting anyone see your profile unless they actually match you. That's a great bonus if you don't want to feel like a piece of meat being picked out at the market on superficial qualities like looks (not that that's not important, but still).

eHarmony also offers some "hand holding" during the communications process, and allows you to go from asking multiple choice question to an email in several steps so you already get an insight to the personality of person you are meeting before you even start using "open communications" as they call it.

Another great feature is the ability to "close" a match. Other dating sites, don't really let you know what happens if the other person decides not to proceed with the relationship. You can imagine the thoughts going through someone's head: "why did she stop emailing me? Did she meet someone? Did she get hit by a truck?" eHarmony allows you to let the person know that you are just not interested in future communications, it hurts a bit, but it's better then not knowing.

What I didn't like about eHarmony: eHarmony's strengths are also its major weaknesses.

For some, the personality profile is just too long to fill out. It takes between 30 minutes to an hour to go through it and you need to pay attention to the details while you do it – and this doesn't even include the time it takes to set up a proper profile. If you are a busy person dedicating a couple of hours to this could be a problem.

The "hand holding" is also quite annoying. It's very hard to convey your personality in this guided process, and sometimes you miss out on meeting great people with a fun personality because they couldn't let it shine through the first 3 steps.

Yahoo! Personals:

Yahoo is another "generic profile" type site. They have less features then match, and don't seem to have as much going for them as match does. The site also doesn't allow you to say too much about yourself (or at least doesn't guide you through the process like match or eHarmony), so if you have some great pictures of yourself, and feel you can "sell" yourself that way, go ahead and post your profile on yahoo…

Myspace.com/Friendster.com:

Myspace is an interesting combination of a "friends/networking" type site where people create their own homepage, to a dating site. it is oriented more towards a younger crowd (teens to early 20's) and It is VERY superficial - people are judged mostly by their photos (and there are plenty of photos out there of guys and girls in skimpy outfits...) the good thing about it, is the price... so far, the site is free, so why not try it out. It does take a bit more work though to create an appealing profile there, so be prepared to download music clips, post cool photos and have some fun stuff to say about yourself.

CHAPTER 6: The "about me" section

Introducing "Bob"

Let me introduce you to a friend of mine, lets call him "Bob". Bob is a typical guy; he has a nice job, makes a good living, has some cool "toys" and overall is an ok guy. Actually, I know many "Bob"s... "Bob" is the personification of a bad profile...

So what makes a profile a "Bob" profile and what makes it a good profile?

This is what I would expect to see in a "Bob" profile:

"My name is Bob. I'm an accountant for a large firm. I specialize in international taxes.
I drive a BMW, and make a good living. I'm really funny, and easygoing, and I like to have fun. I enjoy long walks on the beach, and hanging out and watching DVDs with friends"

If you're still awake, you'll agree with me that while this is not a terrible profile (no spelling mistakes, nothing abusive or insane), this doesn't make you want to know "Bob" better. Honestly, unless "Bob" has some incredible pictures on the site, he will not be getting too many replies to his profile (and even then I'm not sure that he'd get past the first few emails, there's only so much a picture can do for you).

Let's look at Bob's mistakes:

When I started this online dating adventure, I though the profile was used to qualify you as a potential match. I'll tell you a secret, it's not...

The profile (like a resume for a job applicant) is used to DIS-qualify you as a potential match!

I've watched quite a few women browse match.com and the other dating sites. I also talked to countless others about what made them choose a certain profile and reject another. And the overwhelming answer was that if the profile is boring, they will not consider the person as a potential match. Most popular sites have thousands of people on them and it's very easy to stop reading the profile after the first paragraph and move on to the next person. So you gotta keep things interesting!

Another important thing I discovered is that women and men speak in different languages...

I bet you're saying "what do you mean?! They both speak English!", although it's true on the surface, there is a much deeper communication form going on here. You see, men are ruled primarily by linear & logical thought (e.g. when a guy wants to buy a bottle of vitamin C, he goes to the mall, finds the GNC, goes to the vitamin aisle, gets the bottle, pays and goes back. In and out in about 5 minutes, very linear task completion. He doesn't go "shopping") while women "think" in emotions and more abstract forms of thought (a woman needs to get a bottle of vitamin C, she goes to the mall, she walks past and window shops at the stores on the way to the GNC, going in and out of stores that seem interesting to her and that have things that generate an emotional response from her in their windows, tries on some clothes, shoes, purses, jewelry etc. gets to the GNC, chats with the cute sales guy, buys the vitamins, walks back to her car while repeating the same patterns above, 4 hours later, she gets home. This is a simplification of an actual event that happened to me once... ;).

The lesson here is that if you want to attract women online, you have to learn to communicate with them in their type of language. I've seen guys TRY to do this. They copy and paste poems in their profile, write about how they like long walks on the beach, sunsets and other clichés they think will work, but that is not genuine... later on in this book you will learn a bit more about communicating in a genuine way that touches women on a deeper level then just writing a list of qualities that represent you.

The best way to learn "girl speak" is to go out there and read women's profiles. When I started out, I read a few hundred profiles (make sure that if you are "copy pasting", you read profiles of girls in a different city, it's kinda embarrassing if you get caught plagiarizing from the girl you are trying to meet by that same girl) and found some great ways to communicate the qualities I had to offer in "girl speak".

Back to Bob...

Bob starts out by telling us his name. That's nice, but doesn't add much to his personality. Remember, you're not writing an essay or a letter, the profile is meant to help you convey your personality to your potential matches.

Now, Bob is an accountant, I chose this extreme because of the feelings it conjures up in people's minds when they think of it, but honestly, most jobs do not sound amazingly exciting to most people even if they are exciting to you. If you don't hold a job that conveys either high status (like doctor, lawyer etc), or great excitement (like alligator hunter, professional stunt man etc) I would not mention my job in the "about me section" (besides, most profiles have a "career" section, why waste valuable profile space on something that will appear later on anyway?!).

One more thing to be said about mentioning jobs in a profile; even if you do have a great job that conveys social status or excitement, you should not mention it as a fact (i.e. don't say "I am a doctor") this will be perceived as bragging and will lower the value of the rest of the things you have to say. What you can do to convey your job if it's really important to you is say something like "I really like to unwind after a long day at the hospital with a good game of racquetball" or something like that. This way, you're not saying anything about your job, but it is implied that you work in the medical field.

(TIP: this type of sentence could also raise your value if you are not doctors but work at the hospital in other jobs, but you should be prepared to handle the disappointment that comes from finding out that you are not Dr. Drake Ramorè - brain surgeon to the stars, but Mr. Jones, the guy who empties the bedpans... if you can handle this and remain honest about your job in later communications, then you might choose this way of writing a profile)

Another thing you should avoid is "resume"ing your profile. No one cares about where you lived when you were growing up, where you worked as a teenager, or what your last 3 jobs were. Save that for later when you're already getting to know the person, not for the initial phase when you are trying to create interest.

Back to Bob. Talking about the car you drive and the money you make is a total turn off - Especially if you try to brag about it.

This reminds me of a time I was driving in the Silicon Valley (I only had a rental car, so nothing to brag about there... :) and was following a guy in a red Porsche through traffic. He was feeling on top of the world, his top down, music blasting from the stereo, eyeing the girls walking by on the street with a "look at me and my fancy car" look. But then, a red *Ferrari* pulled up beside him... you could actually see the look on his face when he saw that car... soon after, the music on the stereo was turned down, he no longer tried to attract any attention to himself an pulled out of the main road to a side street...

My whole point in this is that some things you think are great and worth bragging about, aren't really so to other people, so no bragging about "things" and that includes the car you drive, the money you make, the boat you own etc...

It would probably not be a good idea to use a story to convey these things too (e.g. "I just got back from the Ferrari dealership, and went to see my accountant about the $20 million investment I just made, and while I was sitting there, his secretary spilled coffee all over my brand new Armani suit..." yeah, you see what I mean...

Bob is making a critical mistake that I've seen appear in countless profiles! I can't emphasize this enough and if there is one more thing that you learn from this book then this should be it! DO NOT USE ADJECTIVES TO DESCRIBE YOUR PERSONALITY!!!
If you say you're funny, but there is nothing funny in your profile, then you're not funny... If you say you're fun loving, but there is nothing indicating that in your profile, then you're not fun loving... You get the point...

This goes back to communicating in a woman's language, the key here is to steer away from the logical, and try to generate an emotional response to what you say.

It's always better to SHOW a quality then just WRITE it. If you want to convey humor, write something funny in your profile (no knock knock jokes please ;) If you want to convey that you love animals, talk about your pets, or put a picture of yourself with a pet in the picture section (more on that later). If you want to convey that you're fun, talk about a fun experience you've had, etc.

The best way to convey a personality trait in a profile is tell a story about it. For every quality you want to convey, tell a small story. E.g. I want to convey that I am a good cook:

"I love to explore new restaurants, the new flavors and tastes this town has to offer seem endless, but the very best meals have always been in my kitchen where I always know the menu"

Compare this to the emotional response that "I'm a great cook" gets you and you'll see what I mean.

As with all rules, there are exceptions, don't try to use the "about me" space to tell your entire life story, and use little stories for each detail, you can list some qualities as adjectives, and you can brag a little, but make sure that that's a small part of the section. Dedicate most of it to conveying qualities in the form of small stories.

Template 1: Sample template for the about me section
1st paragraph: A quick catchy line (in "girl speak" if possible) summarizing why you are here, and then one or two stories about yourself that convey the main qualities you have. 2nd paragraph: Now this is very important: make sure you include humor in your profile. A funny profile goes much further then a "deep" profile. Make sure your humor is not self depreciating, or insulting. Another thing you can use in this paragraph is a challenge to her (when I say challenge I don't mean - "set high standards that a woman has to meet based on the negative past experiences you've had" – I mean that you should give her a chance to prove herself to you – e.g. if you are talking about your love of Italian food, you can say "and if you know some exceptional Italian restaurants around here, you'll get a prize!". This gives her something to talk about in her email to you and

forms some sort of bond between the two of you if you have that thing in common.

3rd paragraph:

Here you talk about what you are looking for which leads us to the next chapter...

Chapter 7: "What am I looking for?"

In The "What I'm looking for" section you have an X number of words to describe what you are looking for in a woman, and you have to verbalize something so fluid and emotional in a way that makes sense to every single person who reads it. But ok, I guess it's there so we have to discuss it...

Now that you've completed exercise 2 (in part 1 of this book), you should already have a pretty good idea of what you are looking for. Should you use that precise description on your profile to describe your ideal mate? Probably not...

The problem is that most people don't know themselves well enough to be able to realize what qualities they have or lack. E.g. most guys think they have a good sense of humor, but adding a smiley face to the end of a sentence doesn't make it funny, right? Just go out there and read some of the profiles that say "I'm funny and have a great sense of humor" I can guarantee that 7 out of 10 of those profiles won't even generate a smile from you...

Furthermore, your idea of what a certain quality is, could be very different from what other people think, e.g. your idea of an adventurous woman could be so someone who likes to go BASE jumping on weekend (for those who don't know, BASE jumping is parachuting off a stationary object – **B**uildings, **A**ntennas, **S**pan (bridges and such) and **E**arth (cliffs, mountains etc.) , but her idea of adventurous, is taking a new route to work every now and then, just imagine the surprised look on her face when you show up to your first date with a tightly packed parachute...

So what should you do?
The best approach to the "What I'm looking for" section is to create a certain situational/emotional context in it and derive the

qualities from there. What do I mean by that? Since there is a wide range for every quality, you should try to generate a visual of a situation or an emotion that speaks of the quality you are looking for – e.g. if you are looking for a sense of humor, but not dry humor, and not cynical humor, you could say, "I'd love to spend my Saturday mornings with you watching cartoons". This generates an image of silliness and childlike fun, and people who fit that description would know what it means. Another example would be if you are looking for someone who knows how to cook, you could say "I want someone who can cook" but that could land you someone who's idea of cooking is warming up a microwave dinner. A better way to say this is "I would really enjoy sharing the smell of freshly baked bread while we spend an evening slicing and dicing vegetables for your signature soup recipe".

Try to avoid lists in this section (i.e. don't say "I'm looking for someone tall, beautiful, smart, rich, blah blah blah...."). Those don't tend to read well, and make people lose interest. The brief story approach works here as well. You can mention things you like to do and share with your relationship partner, emotions that you'd like to feel, and you could even list qualities, but not in a dry list format – e.g. "I'm looking for someone who can carry an intelligent conversation and yet be silly and fun."

Chapter 8: The Picture

Pictures are a sensitive topic. There are some people who don't mind their face being plastered on the internet for all to see. But for many, the online dating experience is revealing enough as it is and they don't really need to have 40 million people staring at their mug shot. There are some ways to make this easier though.

How do you choose your best picture?

I had this one picture I really liked, I took it on a trip to Barcelona, where I had a great time, and I had associated the fun time and positive emotions I had during that trip with that picture. I decided to use that as my main picture. Needless to say, I didn't get too many responses. That is when I decided to try and figure out how to optimize the picture I use.

Exercise 3: Picking the best picture

Step 1:
Find at least 5 pictures of yourself that you like and 5 more that you think are "just ok".
Make sure those pictures are taken from different angles, in different locations, have different lighting and shadows, and include different people if you choose to use group photos. This will allow you to present yourself in different settings and not have all the pictures be from that one party when you got so drunk and thought you were the most gorgeous creature on earth...
If you don't have 10 **recent** pictures of yourself, go out and take some. More about "picture ethics" later on...

Step 2:
Show those 10 pictures to at least 4 friends, try to make sure that the majority of the people who see them are in the target audience (i.e. if

you are trying to attract beautiful women, show those pictures to beautiful women, not your mom, or your buds from college. Women and men look at pictures in different ways (just FYI, ask a man what he sees when he looks at a model in a magazine glamour shot, and he'll talk about the model, ask a woman what she sees looking at the same shot, and it will be what she is wearing).

Now you've gotten one set of opinions on what a good picture is.

Step 3:
Go to a picture ranking site (there are a few popular ones out there like "amihotornot.com" and "myspace.com") and post those pictures there.
Granted, this is not the most scientific way to go about this, the people who rank your picture could range from 13 year old boys, to 60 year old women, but once you get to 100 or so votes (and this should take less then 3 or 4 days in most cases) you will have a good sample of what's a good photo.

Step 4:
Post the top picture (or pictures) that ranked the highest in steps 2 and 3. If there is a significant difference between the 2 methods, try posting both of them and see what happens.

Step 5:
Fortunately, you picked 10 pictures you can use, so experiment. If the first picture doesn't bring good results, try another one. It's not likely (although it is possible of course) that the first person that sees your profile will be the love of your life, so you've can tweak your profile and photos as time goes by.

Some people have asked me about "glamour shots" taken by professional photographers. Most glamour shots don't resemble the "real you". If the photographer is good, then you will look much better then you do in reality, add some Photoshop touch ups, and you've got a whole different person, you will most likely attract more responses with a glamour shot, but your first meeting will most likely have some disappointment attached to it.

What constitutes a good photo?

Obviously the most important thing is to look good in a photo. I have some great photos of me climbing the Great Wall of China, but I look like someone who's climbing the Great Wall of China, and not at my best.

Always smile! The sexy pouty "blue steel" look works sometimes, but a smile always carries more Weight.

If you have any interesting photos, then use them, there is nothing more intriguing then seeing a person in an interesting photo and wanting to ask them what the story behind that photo is. Some examples are – you with a celebrity, with a cool animal (I've got one kissing a beluga whale! That makes a great conversation starter ...), in an interesting place, doing something funny (funny not stupid... so no silly faces in pictures please), wearing an interesting costume and the list goes on...

Another great type of picture is an action shot, of you doing something, and even better, doing something with other people. Pictures of you at a party with lots of friends are always good. Pictures taken on trips or with family work for this as well. Just make sure that you don't use too many group photos and not enough individual photos, there were times where I thought I was meeting one member of the group and ended up meeting another...

A question I hear a lot "I look really good without a shirt, it shows off my body in a great way, why not use that, I'll get tons of responses"? That's true, you will get tons of responses, but those will be from women who haven't even read your profile and are mostly interested in the body they see in the picture, and not the person behind it. If you are looking for a fling, and just some short term fun, then go ahead and get a bigger mailbox because those emails will come in, just be prepared to learn about the more perverted side of online dating...

How many pictures should I post in my profile?

Pictures, like the profile are a great way to disqualify a potential mate. Every additional picture you add is one more opportunity for the girl on the other side of the computer screen to find something wrong with the way you look. I've seen profiles with 15 or more pictures, which were all great except that one photo at the end which made the person look bad in my eyes, and I felt I had to move on and not contact them (superficial, I know, but that's how this works. Girls do that too... I've seen it happen many times...)

So what's the right answer? I'd go with anywhere from 0 to 3 (0 you ask? Yes, see later on in this chapter...) this should give the viewer an opportunity to get a good look at you, without having too many opportunities for disqualification.

One last thing about pictures... I've seen plenty of pictures online in which the person is holding a baby/playing with a child/any other kid related photo. These types of photos can be a double edged sword, so be careful. If it's your child you are playing with, then fine, no problem, that child is part of your life. But if it's a stranger/relative's child, then the initial instinct of the viewer will be "oh, he has a kid" with all the negative (and positive) implications of single parenthood. If they like you enough, they might read your profile and see that you don't have kids and you are just showing your nurturing side, but more often then not, you will be disqualified for no real reason.

Picture Ethics:

Ethics? What does that have to do with online dating?

I know we are all responsible adults and that you bought this book to learn about online dating and not what is right or wrong to do, but ethics have everything do with maximizing your online dating experience.

One of the most painful things that I've experience is showing up at a first date, and realizing the person I've been communicating with, is not who I thought she was, I couldn't hide the disappointed look on my face and I know she felt it as well.

In my opinion, an un-ethical photo is one that does not reflect the real you. Obviously, some people look a bit different in real life then in their pictures, so you can use your judgment on this one and not resort to the latest facial recognition software, but use common sense on this.

Some examples of un-ethical postings:

- If you post a picture of you from 10 years ago, 40 lbs ago, or 6 hair lines ago
- If you post a picture of someone else, or use someone else's picture to create attraction (like in that movie with Steve Martin and Queen Latifa, where she appeared in the background of the picture being led in handcuffs into a police car while an attractive blond was in the foreground of the photo...)

I once met this girl, who apparently was an excellent photographer. She made incredible use of light and shadow to hide her worst features and enhance her best features. When I met her, I was shocked to see that she's doesn't look at all like the person she presented herself as. Trying to start a relationship with a lie like this isn't the best thing to do, so unless you have an incredible personality and the person you meet is very forgiving, try to stay honest with the pictures... I will talk about honest communications a bit more in the advanced techniques section.

What to do if you don't have a good photo?

If you simply cannot find a good photo of yourself, or just don't look good in pictures, there is a solution...

I've had my profile up while I was going through some changes in my life (good ones...) but my most recent picture was one where I was 30 lbs over my current weight and didn't reflect how I looked. So I decided that until I take new pictures, I'll take my photo off.

Surprisingly, that had a minimal effect on my success. Yes, there are girls out there who judge you solely by your photo, but if you write good emails and have a great profile, you could easily do without a photo. I've seen this happen with several friends of mine who decided to go without one. They've been doing very well despite the fact that they don't have a photo posted.

Going without a photo is definitely an option that you can consider. You will be getting less responses, but if you are shy, or prefer not to post a photo (I've met some women who work in mental health and in teaching and they preferred to keep their photos off so their clients/students won't recognize them) then try it out and see if you get good results.

Chapter 9: Profile miscellaneous and advanced technique

Ok, this section comes from my personal bag of tricks. These are advanced techniques, and although they are not "fair play" I consider them to be on the ethical side of things since they do reflect your true personality.

How to get an edge on most other guys using online dating:

I mentioned earlier that I did some experimenting with match.com to figure out how it works, this was not only for scientific purposes, but also to learn more about the "market" I'm in. call it competitive intelligence if you will....

I set up a "girl profile" (using a glamour shot of a girl from another country, and some made up content), and then watched the emails that came in. I used the material I got to differentiate myself from the other thousand of guys out there...

You see, when a girl sets up a profile, the feeding frenzy starts (this is more true in larger cities then in small towns). My "hot girl" profile got dozens of responses from guys who said the same boring things (more on how to write good emails later in this book). I used those emails in two ways - first, I learned to **never** say those things, and second, I used their content to make fun of them when I wrote my emails to the women I was interested in...

Don't forget to delete the "girl" profile when you are done, we don't want hundred of fake girls out there distracting everyone's attention from the real people on the site...

Honesty in communication:

Lying is a difficult subject, I'm sure many of you are saying that people should be completely honest in their profile, but face it, people aren't completely honest in life, and sometimes a small white lie doesn't really have any significance in the grand scheme of things, but can make or break an initial response that would lead to a great relationship.

Age: if you are in your 50's and you say you are 20, that's not a little white lie... but if you are 35 and you say you are 34, that's not too bad. I would be ok with 1-4 years over or under your real age. Some people cut off their searches at certain milestones (like women under 30, men under 35 etc...) And you should be ok with a 1 or 2 year difference.

Body type: that's a tricky one as well... I've met some women whose idea of slender was not, how shall I say it delicately? Not what society considers slender...

Remember, the bigger the lie, the bigger the look of disappointment will be on the other person's face when you meet. But there is some range for you to maneuver in this area - e.g. if you are a few pounds overweight (a FEW pounds) you could easily pass as "about average", if you exercise regularly, you could put down "athletic" even though we all really know what that means. Just make sure you back this up with a great personality, or you will be wasting a lot of your time on 1st dates...

The "little details" like income, likes and dislikes, education, etc:

In my opinion, these are not the most critical for a first meet to go well, so bending the truth on them could work. Now, if the only thing you have in common with a person is your love of snowboarding (and you don't really snowboard), well, you could see where I'm going with this....

Some people do put a lot of importance on those details, so again, it's a judgment call if you want to stretch the truth, or outright lie about them.

Other profile tips:

Don't be extreme:

I've seen some products out there that say "be the bad boy" or "be very romantic". From my experience, profiles that are solely based on extreme qualities don't work; they only attract other extreme personalities. In this case, you should use that advice (if you choose to) as a spice. What do I mean by that? Pepper is a great thing, it makes food taste better, but you wouldn't want to eat it as the main course... when you write the profile, be yourself, and spice it up with the qualities you want to represent.

Stay positive:

I've seen so many profiles of people talking about what they hate, what their ex did to them, why this sucks, why that sucks etc... There really is no need for that and it's not attractive.

Talk about the positive things in your life, what you do like, what is great. Remember, positive people attract positive people, and the same goes for negative people, do you want to be in a relationship that is filled with talk about the bad things in life?

Usernames:

Usernames are not super critical, but they do carry some weight in the selection process.

You could always go with the generic username to stay on the safe side (like dan483, or Paul40232) but you could use your user name as a conversation starter as well.

If you have a cool hobby, you could use the username to bring that up (e.g. origamiguy304 ;), I used a very unique username that doesn't really mean anything, and I always got questions like "that's an interesting name, what does it mean" so I had some cool and funny stories to tell about it and that made a difference.

Some things to keep in mind about a profile:
1. Spelling: with the advent of the spell checker, there is no reason why people should have spelling mistakes anywhere on their profile. There are tons of free spell checkers on-line. Use them!
2. Negative language: As I said before negative language is a turn off, save talking about your ex, the problems you're having with your mother, what you hate about the local baseball team etc, for later on in the relationship, the profile is not the place to air your grievances with the world...
3. Openers: Some might find it cute, but I've seen too much of this and it's really annoying... I'm talking about opening your profile with "I really don't know what to say"... yes you do, you just said it...saying it just makes you seem less confidant, less secure, and like you don't really have a personality. The worst type are the profiles who start like that and then go on for 4 paragraphs, I guess you did know what to say after all...
4. Another opener to avoid is "I don't know why I'm here"... did your dog make you do it? Do you type in your sleep and just woke up to find your profile on this site? Yes, you do know why you are here, you are here to meet someone, the purpose of that is for you to decide, whether it's for a long term relationship, or short term fun, but that's why you are here...

5. Bragging is a turn off. Yes, you have a nice car, and you make lots of money, but that's not what's going to make the difference between you being in the "yes" pile and the "no way" pile.

Summary:

The profile is one of the most prominent ways you communicate your personality to the world, so make sure it helps your personality shine. I know you hear this a lot, but be yourself. Actually, be your "best self". Use your profile to make your personality as attractive as possible without embracing the dark side and lying.

Part Three: Locate & IM/eMail

In this part we're going to start taking action! Searching and finding our potential matches, and actually, yes, brace yourself, actually contacting them!!!

I will also teach you how to find the "hidden gems" that are usually left untouched by most searchers and how to maximize the effect of your emails so that the women you are communicating with will HAVE to meet you.

Chapter 10: The Search

Most sites (excluding personality based match sites like eHarmony and Chemistry.com) allow you to customize your search and look for either specific qualities in a person or perform a broad search.

The first thing you need to consider when you search is the location of the person you are looking for. Many sites recommend that you expand your search to your entire state or even country. That's a great idea, if you are willing to enter a long distance relationship.

If you live in a small town, you will obviously want to provide a broader search radius, and most sites allow you to specify the distance you are searching in. if you live in a big city or in a densely populated area, then you might want to start in your city first (I ran the numbers with a friend and we concluded that there are about 60,000 eligible women in my age range in the city I live in, that means that even if I want to meet only 10% of them (I'm picky...:) it will take me **16 YEARS** of going out on a first date every night to meet them all...).

So how do you make sure you don't get inundated by thousands of matches with a broad search, and yet not miss anyone who might be your "one"?

Most of the popular sites have a cool feature that allows you to save your searches. This will be a useful tool to prevent you from missing out on important possible matches.

This is how to do it:

Step 1:

I created a search according to some very general characteristics I defined in the 'what I am looking for" exercise, this was my must have list. For example, at this point of the search, I am only looking for women who don't smoke, don't have kids, live in my general area, and are of certain religious and racial affiliations. Obviously, this led me to find 1000's of profiles that fit my requirements.

I could browse through them all, but that would take too long and would be very inefficient.

I saved the above search as "generic search1" and proceeded to narrow the qualities I'm looking for down further.

Step 2:
Lets say I really like blonde women, but I don't mind redheads or brunettes either. So what I would do in this case is go to my previously save generic search, and add the "blondes" category in the search criteria. Now I only get blond women to appear in my search results, so I have much less profiles to browse through.

Step 3:
I find the profiles I like**, but I DON'T write them just yet**. I save them to my "favorites" first. Then I go back to my generic search, and remove the check mark from "blonds" and search for redheads. Again, I get a smaller number of profiles, and I save the ones I like.

This can be done with any combination of qualities and attributes, and can be repeated over and over to get a broader or narrower set of matches depending on what you like, while not having to deal with 1000's of profiles in one pass.

Ignoring the profiles that will most likely not respond:

When I first started using match.com, I contacted any person that I found appealing, but I didn't get responses from some of the women I emailed. I was a bit frustrated and tried to figure it out, and after reading their profile again I understood why. There is a very important indicator in the profile that tells you when the person was last active (some sites even provide an exact date and time...).

Turns out that the women I contacted and that didn't reply were not active on the site for quite a while. What does this mean? Who knows... they could have found the love of their life, they could have entered a short term relationship (if you are on these sites for long enough, you'll start to see the "regulars", I actually met up with several women that I was in touch with a year earlier and lost contact with them because they entered a relationship), they could have given up on online dating (obviously they didn't have this book to help them out...;) or they could have been abducted by aliens... you never know. In any case, they haven't been on the site for a long time, and that would probably mean they never saw your email.

Most sites allow you to sort your results by activity date, and as a rule of thumb, I probably wouldn't contact anyone who was not active for 2 weeks or more. There are always exceptions to the rule of course, but most times, you won't hear back from them.

Sorting results is another great idea to narrow down the profiles you select. Most sites allow you to sort by location, age, and several other attributes. This allows you to look through the profiles that match what you want most first and then go to the "maybe" list. E.g. you want to meet someone who lives nearby so you don't have to drive too far to meet your potential match, so you sort by distance, you find 30 or 40 profiles that are quite appealing in a 5 mile radius from you. At this point, you don't really need to go any further, but you can if you want to.

How to find the hidden gems:

Most people search the online dating site and make their selection based on the pictures they see. Unfortunately, not all profiles have pictures. Most people discard those profiles to be of "ugly people" or people with something to hide. But that's not always the case.

Many times, those picture-less profiles belong to very attractive women! You can use some of the search attributes to find the attractive and quality women who chose not to put up their picture for various reasons (some have clients/patients that might find them on the site and want to keep that part of their lives separate from their romantic life. Some (mostly very attractive women) were overwhelmed by the quantity of emails and winks they got and by the low quality of most responses and decided to remove their picture and sometimes even the entire profile).

Let's say I'm looking for "model" body type women in a certain age range. I define the age range in my generic search and then go to body type, knowing that models are usually very slender or athletic and tall, I pick those body types alone and define the height I want. Then I go to the other physical characteristics I am interested (like hair length or color), and select those as well. I also uncheck the "photo only" box so I get all the profiles. Now I have a certain amount of profiles, and I check them out - even the ones without the pictures.

The profiles without the pictures should be read very carefully, and once you get better at understanding the meaning of what people say in the profiles you will start to identify patters. For example – I found that most young lawyers are usually very thin, tall and attractive. So I know that a 27 year old woman who is a lawyer usually fits that profile. No need to see a picture and I have nothing to lose by emailing her.

Same goes for women who are young but have a high income, they are usually in very demanding positions and make sure to stay in shape and maintain their looks.

I've had a lot of success with this approach. One of the women I met online that didn't have a picture was my current girlfriend (the keywords that made me contact her were medical profession and athletic body type, she also had a great profile which told me she was intelligent and had a good sense of humor. Oh, did I mention she used to be a cheerleader? ;). Another woman I met online with no picture turned out to be a local celebrity (keywords here were athletic body type, into running and sports (confirms that), and had some interesting stories on her profile), we ended up becoming friends, we hang out every now and then, and she invites me to parties and gala events that I would have never even known of about before.

I've also met exotic dancers, football cheerleaders, women in the entertainment industry, and many other women who wouldn't have been able to deal with influx of emails from loser guys talking about how big of a fan they are of her work and how they'd be so grateful to meet her – therefore, no picture…

I'm not saying that all women without a picture are celebrities or exotic dancers, yet these hidden gems are very common online. They are a bit harder to find, but it will be much easier for you to stand out of the crowd if you email them even though they don't have a picture.

Now you are done with your search and you have a good amount of profiles in your favorites section (I would go for 50-70 profiles for the first time you try this. At worst, you'll get some good practice in writing emails.)

I recommend you go through the list of favorites one last time, and weed out the "weak maybes". If you do this right, you will be getting a very high response rate, and believe me, time management is key to success in this case, you don't want to have to deal with meeting 50 new people in a short amount of time.
Eventually you should end up with 20 to 40 profiles in your favorites that are a strong "yes" for a possible match.

Some things I use to weed out the "losers": multiple spelling mistakes, **too many** references to food/god/or any other indicators to having a one track mind, very short and non-descriptive profiles that show they didn't really put any time into it and are relying solely on their pictures, very negative language, or pictures that are obviously not reflective of their real appearance (e.g. one glamour shot of someone who looks 10 years younger then what their profile says).

Feel free to add anything that you think might raise a red flag in this category, there are plenty of other people on the site and you don't need to get yourself into a relationship with someone who doesn't match what you are looking for or raises your suspicions from the start.

Chapter 11: Communication

Online dating offers two main ways to communicate, the email, and the wink (also called "icebreaker", "flirt" and other names in different sites). Since you don't really meet the girl you are communicating with, and can't use body language, facial expression, voice tones, etc. to convey your personality, this is the only method you have to make the difference between someone who will go out on a date with you, to someone who will delete your email and never give you a second look.

Winking:

The wink is a coward's way out, and it provides very little value (although I've seen it work in the past on rare occasions – see later on in this section).

Winks are usually free, some sites allow a quick pre-scripted text message that was created by the site owners, and are sent to the girl you are interested in. You can compare this to a canned pickup line that you found on the wall of a bar and you plan to use in that same bar to meet women. If the woman is not extremely ugly, she would have already seen that line, heard it from a bunch of losers who tried it on her before you did, and consider your approach to be extremely lame. Unless you are super attractive, or you're the first guy who ever approached her, you won't get the time of day from her and this lame approach will actually lower your value in her eyes.

Same goes for online winks. If you are very attractive in your pictures, she might click and check your profile out and then (if you've followed my advice in the earlier chapters) you might have a chance to save yourself. Also, consider the fact that she is attractive, and many other guys are interested, so she's probably got 100 emails and winks to look at right now, how do you stand out if you didn't say anything besides some scripted line you got off the website?

Since you can use email to convey your personality and create attraction, you should probably cough up the $30 it costs to register to the site (some sites give a free trial period as well) and send an email. it takes some more work, but it's worth it.

Email approaches:

There are several approaches to sending emails:

The "Nuke" approach:

This approach is a mass mail approach directed to hit anyone and everyone you see. What you do here, is have a template email that you use for all women that you communicate with, and solely based on their pictures, you mass email every woman you like. You sort through the responses and look at profiles based on the ones who reply to you.

I've used this method in the past, and gotten some results, but it's not very effective. You usually miss out on some great women who can tell that this is a mass email, and you get some women to respond to you who you would never email if you'd have read their profile.

The "Sniper" approach:

In this approach, you focus on specific women you like, read their profile, and customize and email to each one based on their profiles. Because it is time consuming, you can only focus on a few women.

This method allows you to create very elaborate emails, base them on the woman's profile, and convey your personality in a way that can spark attraction in a woman. All this is true of course if she actually reads your email....

Attractive women get hundreds of emails every week, and they need a way to manage the mass of emails to prevent them from wasting all their time reading emails from loser guys. You might easily be missed that way, and all the effort you made will be overlooked. She might also just not be attracted, unavailable, on vacation for a month or have other issues you don't know about that will cause her to not reply to your email. Since you only contacted a few women, you risk the chance that you will not get any replies. This is very frustrating, and could cause you to abandon online dating if you keep communicating this way. I don't recommend this method either.

The "Matrix" approach

This method allows you to save time by using a template which I will provide soon, and personalize the email while not spending time on reading profiles and writing too much. Use this approach as follows:

If you've followed the previous chapters, you should by now have a group of 20 – 40 profiles saved in your favorites. Start browsing through the profiles and skim over them and the pictures. You should be able to find some keywords that the girl uses, or notice some key features in the photo, you can then use these items to "personalize" the email template. Real life example: one girl said "I have a man in my life, it's my dog snuggles" (or whatever the name of the dog was...), so I used something like "I hope "your man" knows what you are doing on match! I guess this means we're going to have to meet in dark motels and under bridges in the dark of night so he doesn't find out ;)"

All I did was refer to a line she had in her profile, and to a picture she had. This made her feel that I paid great attention to her profile, and formulated an email only for her. In reality, I attached this line to a template I used but personalized it with details from her profile.

The "Matrix" approach is probably the best one to use, it leads to great response rates (I've had times where I got over 80% response rates, if you know anything about direct mail campaigns (which consider a 2% response rate to be good) then you understand what I mean.

Chapter 12: What do I say?

You have 20 – 40 profiles you want to communicate with, but what do you say to them?

This is where our "fake girl" profile comes to the rescue again (I think I'm starting to fall in love with her, she's just so helpful... ;)

By now, your "fake girl" should have gotten several dozen emails. I'm willing to bet that they breakdown something like this:

40% - "hey babe, what's up?"
30% - "wow! You are so beautiful. Can I take you out some time"?
10% - a 5 page emails describing every single thing the guy ever did in his life from birth to this moment.
10% - guys talking about themselves and how they can make her happy if she'd only write back.
5% - 3 liners filled with spelling mistakes and grammar errors.
4% - cool guys who read this book and know what they are talking about.
1% - this is the "bonus" section – if you live in a large enough city or metro area, you will see them, these are the perverts, freaks and other weirdoes proposing to do all sorts of nasty things to the poor girl/proposing marriage/ offering to pay her money and meet them when their wives are out of town/ etc... This is the darker side of online dating, but attractive women get these emails too...

I want you to be in the 4% who actually know what to say and how to convey their personality...

Once you've read these emails, you will have plenty of material to make fun of in your email.

Template 2: First email template

Hey there *[insert her username here]* (don't assume her real name is the same as her username (e.g. if her username is alice23423 don't assume her real name is Alice, she might just be a fan of Alice in wonderland – using her real name give a "stalker" feel to your email)

[This is where you inset your personalized line/lines – keep it short no more then a paragraph]

[Now for a quick compliment – never compliment her looks, in fact, use her looks to disqualify her. She gets "you're so beautiful" emails all the time... e.g. "I'm not really into blondes, but I read your profile and it looks like you've got a great personality and not just a pretty face"]

[this is where you make fun of the content other guys send in email – e.g. "I can imagine you now, sorting through 5000 emails a day from all sorts of loser guys talking about finally moving out of their mom's basement and how they just divorced their 8th wife"
– feel free to exaggerate here, it's funny... but keep it short - no more then a paragraph]

[now, a little bit about you – not too much, you want her to read your profile, I use 2 lines about my age, having my life together, and telling her I'm interesting and funny (which I proved in the previous paragraph and in my profile)]

[I don't ever ask women on a "date", I'm qualifying them to see if we can be friends, so I tell her something like "you seem cool, I bet you'd make an interesting friend"]

[call to action – now we tell her what we want her to do – e.g. "how about we meet for coffee or a drink sometime next week", and I *always throw in a challenge - e.g. "if you can handle some interesting conversation of course..."]*

[don't put in any of the formal letter endings, you're not writing a business letter, just sign your name – real name, and put down your email in case she wants to reply to you directly, or her subscription is running out. Some sites block email addresses from communications, so you can circumvent their mechanism by using something like: joe2 at (y)a(h)o(o) dot c/o/m. feel free to experiment with this using your girl profile as a test subject and see what she gets.]

If you still doubt the power of this template (O ye of little faith... ;) check this out –

Below is just a small sample of email replies I got after sending out my first email using the template. Remember - I didn't have a photo posted, and I am very picky about the women I contacted - so these are very attractive and intelligent women answering my email. Obviously, I removed any identifying info from these emails, but these are actual emails I got! I included my comments in *Italics*.

"You are pretty good, you had me cracking up with the first email. So, you must be a good looking guy, with all the crazy stalker women hiding outside your place :) *[in my profile I tell women that I didn't post a picture because I'm afraid they will fall in love with my pics and start stalking me]* Hey, well, at least we have something in common...of course I don't have any crazy women stalking me but I have had my fair share of the stalker type men! We just have too much going for us, it is hard being good looking and brilliant isn't it?
I love to laugh, it is one of the best feelings you can experience. I enjoy life to the fullest and love meeting people with the same outlook...and guess what, it could be your lucky day...you may just be one of those new people in my life :) So, in response to your "if you

can handle it" comment, the real question may be can you handle it? *[Look how she is trying to qualify herself and explain/excuse how good she really is - women don't do that unless they are really interested and see you as high value to them]* I am alot to take in, all of this fiery spirit I have about me. :) You sound great, glad you decided to send me an email, I look forward to talking more, meeting up and figuring out why you have all these women falling for you! (My personal email is ********@hotmail.com)
Take care,
Nichol"

So this girl, who is a very attractive redhead (if we ever meet in person, you will have to buy me a drink and I will share all the "hot crazy redhead" stories I have...), took quite a lot of time to write me almost half a page long email and is trying to convince me that she and I have a lot in common and I should "choose" her, she also gave me her personal email... and all this from 3 paragraphs of text I sent her...

"You sound pretty darn funny. Are you just a figment of my imagination after a long new years weekend? Oh yeah, happy new year by the way. A cup of something delicious and lots of laughter!! I am up for it.
Natalie"

Now all that is left is to figure out the logistic and I have a date...

"Okay - I have to say this is the first email I've answered where there is no photo posted - but your email (and profile) cracked me up.
Please tell me you are not serious about stalkers. Has this happened to you? Also women who tell you they love you after a few dates? *[Actually, I had a woman fall in love with me while we were emailing...]* I thought that only happened on TV.

I've gotten a few strange emails (one dude who asked if he could rub my feet and another who was in town from Saudi - gave me his hotel phone number and ROOM NUMBER ... oh my ... coco loco!)
Laura
P.S. - what is the significance of your screen name? Mine, sadly, is not original!"

At this point I already have her interest and she is asking me some questions to get me into a conversation, if your online game is good enough, you should be able to get a woman like this to go out with you in the next 2 emails.

"Luckily, I don't get too many losers as bad off as you picture them to be! I do have my share of weirdos contacting me though. Sometimes I am flypaper for freaks. A cup of something delicious sounds good to me.
Kelly"

"do you mind if we talk on the phone, can't bother with the computer much longer. If you give me your number, I'll call *[and she did]*. Don't worry I am completely normal! Julie"

This is another variation, some women are not very comfortable going out with a guy they just met online (rightfully so... there are lots of weirdoes out there...), so they go for the phone call first. In this case I gave her my # and she called, I will talk a bit more about this in the next sections.

"I usually don't respond to emails without a profile picture posted...but your profile seems very interesting and my curiosity is piqued. I enjoy meeting new people especially those with a sense of humor and you seem to have one.
As you suggested and if you're interested, let's meet for a cup of hot chocolate. Hope to hear from you."

I emailed her, and she then is asking for my "permission" – "if you're interested, let's meet" – the frame is now reversed, I no longer need to convince her to go out with me, she is the one hoping that I agree to go out with her (this woman was very successful, intelligent and beautiful, she's not someone with low self esteem)

Last one –
"Well, you certainly have my attention...and you made me laugh (that is a big bonus). I have to say that your profile is intriguing... Hmmm. I think you are someone I need to meet. Also, I am curious to see if I can guess which school you attended. *[I make some comments about my school in my profile that always makes them want to try to figure it out - always encourage some mystery in your profile]* But first, there are some important questions I must ask: what kind of puppies do you have? where is your favorite place to snow board? what is your favorite mexican food?"

Notice how she's trying to get me invested in a conversation with her by asking all those questions, this is usually what loser guys do when they meet an attractive woman. I guess I turned her into a loser guy... ;)]

Qualities the email should display:

Your email is a window to your personality. The girl will most likely respond to it if you convey qualities that women are attracted to:

Confidence: you must show that you are confidant that you are the reward, and that you assume she is already attracted to you and will definitely want to respond to your email. Don't say things like "I hope you'll like my profile" or "or please write me back" or best of all "eagerly waiting your response" yeah, that's a good one... assume that she is interested in you and all that is left is to figure out the logistics of your first meet.

Never apologize for stuff that you think might be wrong with you. E.g. if you are 5'8 and she says she is looking for guys taller then 5'9, then don't say "I know you are looking for guys who are over 5'9, but I am 5'8 and if I wear shoes I'm easily and inch taller"... the girl probably noticed that you are 5'8, and nothing you say will change that. If you are confident, funny and cool, she will easily overlook that. You bringing it up again, makes her focus on it and makes it a stronger negative point in her mind.

Humor: if you can make a girl laugh, you are way ahead of most guys. I've seen girls communicating, dating and sleeping with guys who have red flags saying "do not date this guy" splattered all over only because they were really funny...

Now, when I say humor, I don't mean that you need to include knock knock jokes in your email... I'm talking about playful humor, tease the girl, make light fun of her. E.g. sometimes girls email me the same first reply twice just because they clicked the send button twice, so I accuse them of being in love with me and that they will become my stalkers... they know I'm kidding and I'm teasing them, and they love it and write back to deny this...

Oh, and putting a smiley face after something doesn't make it funny. Your humor needs to be slightly arrogant, and playful.

High social value: This is true for both the profile and the emails, if you can add social value to a girl's life (knowing cool places to go, doing cool things, etc...) then you will have a huge advantage over guys who talk about movie nights and cuddling on the couch.

When do I send out an email?

Some sites allow you to see when a user is online. You might think that that is the best time for you to send out an email and have it read, but that's not the best strategy for the first email. I've found that the best time to send out a first email to a woman is not when she is online, but before that, at a time when she is least occupied.

That would usually be sometime early in Sunday afternoon; she's done with her weekend activities, gotten back from brunch/church/ etc. and opens her computer and can devote the most attention to your email. Not that you can't send an email at any other time, but that is the best time to get a response.

What do I put in the subject line?

Subject lines are the first part of the email the girl sees when you write to her. If you use them correctly, you can increase the chances of her opening and reading your emails.

I've experimented with a bunch of different subject lines, and this is what I've found:

I've been successful with using a simple "hey there" in the subject line. It shows that you aren't trying too hard to be funny or overly creative and that you are cool.

I've had even better results using the matrix approach for subject lines. What I did is find interesting things in her profile, and commented on them in the subject line. E.g. one girl talks about how busy she is and how she has trouble scheduling time to meet people – so in my subject line I put "have your people call my people". This makes me different from all the other losers who write stuff like "wow, your so cute", or "I like *(insert noun here)* too".

Another great idea for a subject line is to tease or challenge her. Using a challenge or a tease will practically make her open the email and want to respond to you. Use the matrix approach on this one as well and pick an element from her profile that you think you can use.

E.g. if she talks about Mexican food in her profile and how much she loves it, you can say "I can't believe you like Mexican food!!!" – She will feel that she must open your email, to see what you mean by that, and why you "have the balls" to challenge her. Obviously, you don't need to say anything about Mexican food in your email, the subject line is just to get her to open it.

If you are going to challenge her, avoid very personal subjects like religion, family and politics, those will just get her defensive. Keep things light, playful and funny. E.g. don't say "I can't believe you believe in god?!"...

How long should a first email be?

Imagine you are an attractive woman joining an online dating site and getting 100s of emails in the first 3 days. Would you really spend time reading pages and pages of emails that guys send you? Probably not. When you set up your "fake girl" profile, you will see guys spend hours writing pages of text to a woman who will never read it. In my experience, you should keep your email as close as possible to my template. I've gotten great results sending an email that is something like 7-10 lines long, and that will work for you too once you get good at this. You can send a longer one, but don't go over 20 lines, she won't read it.

Chapter 13: The email exchange

Now you've sent out 20 – 40 first emails. All you have to do is wait...

Some sites allow you to view who's seen your profile, some even tell you when they did that. You can use that to track if the girl read your email and checked your profile or not. This feature can be a double edged sword though, because it also allows the woman to see when you've viewed her. Many people who go online tend to get obsessive about this and usually check how many times the person they emailed checked them out, when was the last time they were online, and then wonder why they haven't responded. That's not a very healthy attitude - you can't control what other people do, and sometimes people just take their time responding to emails. Obsessing like this wastes time and energy and worse, if she can see you checking her profile all the time, you could get put in the "obsessive stalker" bucket.

If you do feel the need to obsess like that, you could keep a separate document where you track usernames, and then while you are logged out (make sure you are logged out!) do a username search on that username. Make sure you search for someone else before you log in because some sites log you in directly to the last profile you were looking at).

Tracking & managing emails:

At first, you might not get too many responses so you won't feel the need to track and manage your emails, but as you keep tweaking your first email you will see your response rate go up and you WILL need to track and manage your communications.

I used a spreadsheet, and divided it into 5 sections: emails sent, follow up, closed, communicating, and date pipeline. This way, I know who I sent emails to, so I don't resend the same email to later (although you can successfully resend the exact same email to the same girl a few months later, it's probably not a good idea to do it in very short intervals) I use the follow up section to track my follow up emails.

Sometimes, a girl would be genuinely interested in you but is so overwhelmed by emails that she doesn't respond, or even read, your emails. Most guys just assume she's not interested and move on (or keep sending her emails saying something like "why don't you answer me?!")

If there are girls that I am really interested in and I have some free time to fit them in my schedule, I usually follow up after 4 or 5 days by saying one something like this:

> **Template 3: Follow up**
>
> Hey [*insert her username here*]
>
> [*This is where you tell her that you emailed her in the past (don't give a specific date, say something like "a few days ago") , you should also include a funny sentence teasing her about where she's gone like* "have you been having so much fun with your dog that you forgot to email me back?" – *this sentence needs to be related to her profile*]
>
> [*Now you give her one last chance and make her feel like she'll be losing something if she doesn't contact you* – "Well I figured I'd give you one last shot. When I read your profile I thought you'd make a cool friend, am I wrong?"]
>
> [*The next sentence is a logical appeal to show her how small the "risk" is of communicating with you* – "we're both on the site to meet someone, and I think it would be a real shame for both of us if we never spoke."]
>
> [*Finally, you sign off by talking about things you have in common or talking yourself up (not bragging!) and telling her to email you, then just sign your name and give your email address*]

The closed section is for girls who either responded with a "not interested" email, or that didn't respond at all after follow up. This doesn't mean that it's over. I've had several occasions where girls sent me a not interested email, or even completely vanished, and I still emailed them a few months (or even a year) later and we met in person and got into a relationship. Sometimes the timing is just wrong, and sometimes they don't even remember you emailed them in the past...

The "communicating" section is self explanatory. This is where I list girls I am actually communicating with and what stage we are at (see next chapters for communication stages).

The date pipeline section is used to solve a "high quality" problem. I use this section to line up my dates, and track the girls I have dates set up with. This is critical so that you don't end up setting up a date with more then one woman at the same time. I also use this section to track my skill progression and document what I've learned in each interaction.

There were times where I seemed to be messing up date after date, and then suddenly I looked at my learnings and discovered a pattern that recurred, once I corrected that mistake, I was on a roll again! Fortunately for you, you have access to these learnings in the book.

Chapter 14: The Sam Stone™ email method

Now you've got a batch of women you are corresponding with (out of the 20 -40 emails you've sent you should get about 2-5% to communicate with you initially and that number will quickly rise to about 50-80% within a few months of doing this properly. If you are still stuck at a low percentage of replies, you are probably doing something wrong in the previous steps – review you're Attitude-Profile-Locate-email phases.).

The Sam Stone™ email method:

How many emails are required until you get a date?

I would highly discourage you to get into a lengthy email exchange (unless you are planning a long distance relationship where it's either email or phone and then it's up to you to pick where you are more comfortable). Important rule - **The more you email the girl, the less likely you are to meet her**. Also, the more the two of you email each other, the more a "fantasy" is created in both your minds about each other's personality. These fantasies are not based on real behavior but on how your mind fills the gaps between what you know about the other person through their emails. Once you meet, you will both discover that this fantasy is not real and will most likely be disappointed.

On the other hand, you will have to make the girl comfortable and attracted enough to you to actually agree to go out with you. Initially, you won't have the first steps optimized and you won't be able to get a date based on your profile and your first email.
Another important thing - you are the "reward" remember? - Just because the girl is hot doesn't mean that you will automatically agree to go out with her. She needs to feel like she's worked and made you "willing" to go out with her and still has to prove herself to you.

From my experience, until you are better at online dating, you shouldn't ask a girl out before your 5th email, you should keep on trying to get to know her, and learn more about her while providing fun and interesting conversation to keep her coming back for more.

Once you get better, you should ask a girl out no later then the 3rd email, there is no reason to wait much longer. If you get really good, you will have girls asking you out...

How long should each email be?

After the first email - emails should be no longer then 4 or 5 paragraphs at most.

What should I talk about in my emails?

The best way to make a girl more interested in you is to be somewhat of a challenge – I'm not saying that you need to be a total mystery and not tell her anything and make her feel like she's pulling teeth just to get your name. What I mean is that you need to be a challenge playfully and make it fun for her to "work" to get to know you.

Give her some hints and make her guess something; tease her, play with her.

The points system

I've been very successful using the points system – what I do is reward or "punish" a girl for things she says in email by giving or taking points from her. E.g. she says that she hasn't traveled that much, so I tell her that she loses 50 points for that, and she better be careful because if she keeps losing points she won't get anywhere with me. This also works the other way, so for example when she says that she's a really good cook, I "give" her 5 points. LOL, notice the difference in what I take off and what I give her. She will really get into trying to get more points with you to redeem herself.

This sounds very stupid, but it works... as with any other technique, don't over use it, giving her points for every single thing she says will become annoying very quickly. You can also expand this game and assign value to the points, so let's say 10 points buys her coffee, 30 points buys her cake, and 50 points gets her a kiss. If she likes you, she will try very hard to get to those 50 points...

Doing things for her

Don't go overboard in doing stuff for her. What I mean by this is that you should not show any supplicative behavior that shows that you need to do anything besides being yourself in order to get her to like you.

I've seen guys set up elaborate websites for women, or create online playlists for them with music they might like. It's very sweet, very romantic, but it's something that you do for someone you know.

Any time you go out of the way to please a woman in order to get her to like you, you are lowering your value in her eyes. Would you go out of your way like this for a total stranger? No, and that's what she is right now... once you are dating for a while, you can go ahead and do that, but for now, you haven't even met her in person, for all you know, she might be a 13 year old boy messing with you online, you need to qualify her as to why she is worthy of your time.

Qualifying

Qualifying is another thing to do in initial emails. You need to ask her questions that imply that you are still "considering" her as a possible date.

Say things like "can you cook?" or be funny and use something like "do you make a lot of money? I'm looking for a sugar momma... ;)". Again, remember that you need to keep it playful and funny...

When I started out with online dating I would also qualify girls on their looks. I would tease them on being really scary in person. I would say that the owners of the website asked them to hide their pictures because it was scaring the neighborhood kids if they didn't have a picture posted, or say that her picture wasn't real or too old if they did have one. I decided not to use this type of qualification since it would really hurt a girl's feelings when she actually did send me a real picture of her and I decided she wasn't my type (hence implying that she actually was really scary...). This type of qualification is super powerful though, there were times that I used it, and got girls to send me pictures of them in their underwear, and even naked (or making out with other women, or other naughty stuff), and this is from girls who never even met me...

"Romantic FAQ"

Once you start getting better at this, you will find that most women ask the same questions early on. This is where stock material comes to into play.

Over time, I've developed a collection of answers to frequently asked questions – you can call it a "romantic FAQ"...

I keep it in a file and every time I get asked one of those typical questions like "where are you from", "what do you do for a living" "what do you like to do for fun" I just copy and paste the answer from my file. This is an evolving file of course, so the answers slightly change over time and become funnier and more seductive every time I use them. Once you use online dating for a while, you will also get bored of answering the same question over and over again, and you will start coping and pasting your own stock material.

How do you develop stock material?

When you get started, you will not have any stock material to use, there is stuff out on the internet, but that's not your material and it will feel unnatural to use it.

You should start by honestly answering the questions the girl asks you, with some detail, but not too much, and try to incorporate something funny, playful or challenging in each answer. E.g. when a girl asks "tell me more about yourself" I already have a stock answer ready, it includes a section about me learning something special in Oklahoma 10 years ago, and I tell her to guess what it is. This is not only a challenge for her (and they never guess it...;) but it also gives me a chance later on to tease her on not being good at guessing games, make a bet with her to get her to buy me coffee on our first date (in this case, I am assuming that there will be a first date and making her buy into that assumption as well), or continuing the email conversation by giving her hints and helping her get closer to the answer.

Another great example is when they ask me about my dogs (I mention that on my profile – women usually really like dogs and I often get asked "what kind of dogs do you have").

This is an actually piece of my stock answer for this question –

My dogs? I have a mini Dalmatian and a mini German Shepard.
Now I bet your thinking, "I never heard of those breeds", you're right, I just made them up... they're actually just mutts but that's their main breed and they are small, and I do want them to feel like they are purebred... ;)

p.s. if you just copy this and use this in your emails, I will hunt you down... ok, just kidding... ;)

Once you start getting repetitive questions, start changing your answers slightly to make them funnier or better. You will start getting responses like "LOL! I loved what you said about your dogs...". When you get a few of those to the same answer, you know you got something you can put in your collection of stock material...

Same goes for negative responses. If you try something and you get very negative responses to it, you might want to stop using it...

Don't be discouraged by one or two negative responses, or over excited about one or two positive ones, you could have just been lucky/unlucky with the girls you hit up. Try each piece of material at least 4 or 5 times before you decide to stock or to dump the material you are using.

Once you stock up on enough material, you will be able to answer the first few emails you exchange with a girl in just a few seconds because you already know what you are going to say. I've gotten dates using nothing but stock material, I'd say it took me a few seconds to read the girls' emails, and then a few seconds to copy and paste my stock answers into the reply. So about 30 seconds to get a total stranger to go out on a date, I don't think anyone has ever done something like that in a bar doing pickup...

Email exchange frequency

You will meet many cool girls online, they are going to be attractive and fun and you will want to spend the day emailing back and forth with them, bantering and teasing each other. But don't. A woman needs to feel that you are not readily available for her, that you have other things to do in life and that you are not sitting by the computer hitting the "check mail" button every 2 minutes to see if there is anything new from her (and I know you will be doing that... but still...;) .

I usually do my online dating emails early in the morning. Then get responses during the day and in the evening, and then send out replies the next day. This way, the girl is the one who is anticipating the email from me, and this increases the attraction. I've actually had girls complain when the "morning email" they'd get from me was late or didn't come that day...

This system also evolved naturally around my dating schedule –
- Sunday – send out emails and get responses
- Monday Tuesday Wednesday – communicate and set up dates
- Thursday-Friday-Saturday-Sunday (and on into next week) – go out on dates.

In the past, I preferred to meet girls on weekends because I could fit 3 girls into one day (brunch, afternoon coffee, and evening coffee)X2 = 6 girls in a weekend + 1 on every weekday after that. It's up to you how you construct your schedule.

Moving

Once you spend enough time on a dating site, you will start seeing the same faces over and over again, there will always be new ones, but you will start to notice the "regulars", you don't want to burn yourself out too soon (especially in smaller towns) when you don't have the skills down yet. This is also great method you can use to build stock material and to get some practice when you start out it's called "moving".

No, I don't mean that you need to physically move to a new town, but with a click of a mouse, you can change your location on the dating site, and then you have a totally new set of girls you can practice on without risking any future relationship potential. I don't recommend "moving" to major "player" cities like LA or NY, you might want to start out in smaller, less "sophisticated" cities and practice there. If you do want an advanced class in online pick up, then LA or NY are the place to be, but expect a lot of rejection and competition...

The Sam Stone™ email method is the structure I put together for getting a girl to meet after 3 emails:

First email: Use first email template.
Second email: At this point she will most likely respond with something like "you are so funny" and ask a few questions. You answer some of the questions, don't put too much time into this yet, and then send out a stock question, saying something like "tell me more about yourself" (most girls are not secure enough to come up with their own answer to this question, and usually respond with "well, what do you want to know?", so you need to discourage that by saying something like "and if you say "well, what do you want to know", you lose 50 points!" ;)
Third email: She will reply to you with some info on her, this is great because now you have more material. And she will also say something like "now it's your turn to tell me about yourself"
This email is structured as follows:

Template 4: Third email template

Part 1: here you respond to what she says, you could comment on the cool stuff she did, tease her for something she mentioned in her email, or ask follow up questions.

Part 2: now you use your stock "tell me about yourself" response. I purposely get her to ask this question because it is very broad and open ended. You can tell her about something cool you do for work (make sure it's cool for her as well, Database management might be the coolest thing in your world, but not everyone feels that way), something from your childhood, interesting places you've been, basically anything interesting/fun you can come up with. I use the story of how I came to live in Houston, it has a lot of guessing games, humor and challenges to keep it interesting for her.

Part 3: at this point, you should have enough interest generated to ask her out. If you are a beginner, I would recommend you wait with this part until email #4 so that you can still calibrate your stories in email #3 and know if it's the stories that aren't working or the way you are asking them out.

I usually say something like: "you seem like a cool girl and I'd like to get to know you better, but before I let you take me out for a romantic evening of dancing and dining *(notice that I say "I let you take me out" as if she is the one who is asking me out)*, how about we meet for coffee *(or any other date that comes to mind, see later in the book on how to structure the date)*. That way, if I find out that you are too scary in person and have that stalker look in your eyes, I can say that I need to go mow my sister's lawn and leave (and I don't even have a sister! ;)." *(This is totally outrageous but funny, and you will usually get girls to justify that they are really normal and nice and you should meet them in person...)*

After this email you should know where you stand. If she replies with a "yes, lets meet" (and you will get yes most of the time, once you are good a this) then all that is left is to set up the date.

She could say "no" - that is actually quite rare, even for beginners, what might happen is that she just stops talking to you.

Another possible and annoying answers is "I want to talk to you on the phone first, give me your/here is my number". This is her way of stalling and getting to "know" you a bit better. Honestly, I don't like talking on the phone, I rarely do it with my GF or my closest friends, I just don't like it. I tell them that I don't do the phone thing, and say something like: "I don't really do the phone thing, I'm on the phone all day at work and I find it very impersonal, besides, if I call you, you'll have my number and then you'll start calling me 10000 times a day leaving me 20000 messages about how much you love me and want me! No thanks! ;)"

I exaggerate on purpose to make sure she knows I'm joking. This is a bit of a risk, because if you didn't generate enough attraction you might lose the girl. But if you don't have good phone game, or don't like talking on the phone, then the risk is worth it.

I don't think I ever lost a girl by not talking to her on the phone. I did talk to some on the phone, and it was quite a waste of time because all we did is talk about what we would talk about on the first date anyway, so why waste that time and good quality material on a phone call when you could do it in person and see what the girl is really like?

Once you get good at this, you will see that there are enough girls out there, and if one insists on talking to you on the phone and won't meet you before that, it's her loss. Many women actually prefer to meet in person for the first time without talking on the phone so they can see the "real you" and not have to rely on profile/picture/phone call that don't reflect how you behave in the real world.

Another thing that you might get is "are you on AOL/MSN/ICQ ?" or any other IM system. It is a big mistake to get involved in IM with a girl you met on a dating site and want to meet in person.

First, IM makes you more available. You can ignore the girl, block her, or make yourself invisible to her, but she still feels like she can contact you more often.

Second, like the phone call, it's not the real world. The more you delay meeting her in person, the less likely you are to meet her ever! Later on in a relationship, feel free to call, IM, send letters or whatever, but at this point – you are on the APL-IED method (actually I've got a confession to make, I only used "IM" in the APL-IED method so it doesn't turn into "apled" (pronounced appled) and then I'll have to deal with all sorts of copyright lawsuits from Steve Jobs...;)

Seriously though, the more time you spend in the virtual world, the more virtual you are to her, get to a meeting as soon as possible. I know it's more comfortable to hide behind the phone or IM or email, but face it, you are hiding, you can have as much virtual or phone sex you want, but it's still you doing the "work". The only way to meet women is to actually MEET them...

Back to the emails...

After email #3 and its response, you should be planning a date. Try to schedule it for as soon as possible, so she doesn't forget the attraction she has to you. But don't be too available. If she suggests a day, say you are busy, and suggest an alternative. You can even say you are busy and then when she gets back to you with an answer to the alternative you can say that she's really lucky because your schedule just opened up for that day...

You might be tempted to continue the conversation over the days before your date. Try to keep it to a minimum. She's going out with you already, so anything you say now can only screw it up. Obviously don't ignore her, but make sure to keep communications to a minimum.

Advanced email techniques:

As you start emailing girls, you will notice that their schedules are sometimes very different then yours and that they seem to be busy all the time. Unfortunately, until you meet them and attract them in person, you are just some guy who they are emailing with. Attractive women usually have several of these at a time and even though things seem to be going well with the two of you in email, she might not consider you the most important thing in her life and not reply in a timely manner.

Of course, if she is like clockwork, and replies to every one of your emails immediately, that usually is a sign that she likes you, but some girls are just busy, and even though they like you, they will "forget" to email you. This is also a test sometimes, to see if you will just give up on them, or if you are genuinely interested and will be persistent enough but not too needy.

In any case, persistence is important here. As with the follow up email, you should make sure not to lose communications with a girl for too long. Look at your emailing pattern with her (i.e. how often are you emailing each other) and if she misses more then 2 cycles (if you email once a day and she's silent for 2 days), then send her a follow up email, similar to before, but shorter, something like "hey, did you get my last email? Where did you vanish to? [And here you insert a funny comment on why she must have vanished based on her previous emails - e.g. if the 2 of you are talking about road trips, you can say "did you get lost on one of your road trips? Do I need to send lassie out to find you?"], and then just sign your name.

This should usually generate a response and she will apologize with some excuse to why she didn't reply. If this happens too often, then you might want to cut her off because if she flakes out on emails like this, then chances are high she will flake out on a date, but if it only happens once or twice it shouldn't be a problem.

That being said, don't become an angry (or even a cheerful... ;) stalker! Just because she doesn't answer your email doesn't mean she's not interested, she might be out of town, her best friend might be going through a rough time and she needs to be there for her, or again, the alien abduction thing.... ;) I've seen emails from guys going through a whole range of negative emotions to why the girl didn't answer them while all that happened was that the girl was out of town and didn't mention it to them (the guy went from being cute to being self conscious "are you not answering me because of my looks?" and eventually he started calling her "slut" and ranting about her low sense of morality. Don't be the insane guy. If a girl doesn't respond, follow up, and if that doesn't work, then move on... remember the video game (see chapter 3 if you forgot) ? That's all it is, you shouldn't get all emotional because of it.

Online etiquette

Sadly, online etiquette allows any one of the two communicating sides to just stop and disappear without any explanation. Some sites, like eHarmony, have a "close" feature that at least lets you know it's over, but most sites don't have that.

Personally, I prefer to let the girl know that I am not going to communicate with her anymore. I usually tell her I met someone and we're getting serious, so she doesn't feel bad.

I've actually renewed contact with some of those girls who just stopped communication with me, even a year later, turns out they got back with an old boyfriend, were just on a break from their relationship, or met someone else. It happens. Learn from it, Deal with it and move on.

Some sites allow you to see who's viewed your profile. That's a great feature, but this also means the girl's know who looked at them as well. You don't want to be "stalker guy" who looks at a girl's profile 500 times a day – sometimes you just need to check out her profile to strategize, or just to see her pictures again if you are trying to make a decision about her but you don't want her to know you were there.

The way to work around this is to copy down her username, log out of the site, and do a username search to find her again and check out her profile (if the site doesn't offer a username search, then do a regular search and limit the age range to her age). You won't get all the features the site allows, but you'll still have enough.

Another way to work around this is to use your fake girl profile to look at her. She'll probably wonder why this girl keeps checking her out all the time, but you will be safe...

Scams and how to avoid them:

The internet is heaven for scammers and online dating has not been spared. Currently, there are two major scams that are going around in online dating sites, the Nigerian and the Russian scams.
This is how they work:

An attractive girl either responds to your email, or initiates contact with you. She seems nice, and even though her English is not perfect, she manages to say a lot about herself. Her pictures are "glamour shots" and she looks great. So you email her back.

You exchange emails for a while, and after several emails where you both bare your souls to each other and share your inner most feelings, she will ask you for money in some way. It could be to fly to see her sick mother in Russia or Nigeria, it could be to get an airplane ticket so she can come visit you, or any other reason. The poor hot girl even promises that she'll pay you back once you meet which will be very soon...

Of course that once she gets the money, you will never hear from her again...

Some of these scammers even give you a phone number to call, but unfortunately the "girl" is really busy and never answers...

How to avoid being scammed:

First, never send money to anyone you meet online (of course if you meet the girl of your dreams online, get married, and have 3 kids, you could probably break this rule at that point...;) if she wants to buy a plane ticket, send her to Expedia.com.

Second, in her emails, does she say anything specific to your communications? Or is she just rambling on without answering any of your questions. Scammers usually use canned emails and they don't bother reading yours...

Did she contact you? Is she living in Russia or Nigeria? This is usually a rare thing, watch out if this happens.

If she says she's from your area, does she mention local hang outs? Local culture? Anything local? If she can't point out anything local, then she's most likely not really in your area...

Notice the photos she posts, do they look like they are from the area she says she's from? Pictures of mountains where there should be none, picture of snow in Florida, signs in the background the are not in English, etc...), of course, they could be from a trip she took, but that should raise a red flag and she should be able to explain them.

Of course, there are some really great women from Russia or Nigeria who live in your area and really want to meet you, not all of them are scammers, but I just want you to be aware that this exists and make sure you don't fall for this.

The webcam/porn scams:

Another kind of scam is the webcam/porn scams.

In this scam, a girl emails or IM's you saying how she liked your profile and how she thinks you're cute. She tells you about herself and tells you that she has a website set up where you can learn more (this could be a myspace page or just a random website that looks like an amateur web page). When you go to the site, you will see some text about her, and usually some very suggestive pictures of her in a skimpy outfit.

After the pictures, you will usually see a link saying something like "I have more pictures here, but the guy who runs my server doesn't want to let kids into this site because they are really naughty, so I need to verify that you are really an adult" this link leads to adult verification software that asks for your credit card. I've never gone further, but from what I hear, you get to see her pics/webcam, but you never meet her. Later that month, you get a charge on your credit card.

This is also a great way to steal your identity.

Most women who are legitimately online to meet someone, will not ask you for money, your credit card, or your personal financial info. Don't give those out, no matter how horny or in love you are, and you will be well protected from scams.

Part 4: The Sam Stone™ date method.

"Eighty percent of success is showing up."
Woody Allen

Initially, I wasn't sure if I want to include this part in the book since this is a book about online dating success, not a dating guide. The first date is key to what makes the Sam Stone™ method so powerful and decided to share my secret stash of dating techniques with you.

I've analyzed the dating process and split the date into 4 parts:
1st: The setup and mindset
2nd: The introduction and early part of the date
3rd: Mid date
4th: Ending the date

Mastering these parts will make every date you are on a success and will allow you to cut short a date with someone you don't want to spend time with.

Chapter 15:
The Date - Part 1: Setup and mindset

The first mistake I've seen people who are learning online dating do is to assume continuity of attraction in the transition from online to real world dating, I was guilty of this too.

What I mean is: lets say you meet this great girl online, exchange some emails and get a feel that you really know her and that she really likes you (she could be saying that she thinks you're funny, charming, intelligent, etc, or complimenting you or just outright saying that she likes you...), but when you meet her in person, that chemistry you had online just evaporates and the date becomes awkward and boring.

This happens because attraction online doesn't automatically translates to attraction in the real world. When you talk to a girl online, she gets to sit back in the comfort of her home, sometimes she has a couple of girlfriends there and they help her write the email and enhance the good feelings she has with your communication (I've seen that happen in person), she is responding only to the text you are writing and creating a fantasy in her mind of what you are like in person. When you finally meet in person, there is a whole new set of things for her to respond to; your looks, the place you picked, the loudness/smoke of the place and many other factors that interfere with her ability to create that fantasy in her head again.

She obviously liked you before, so you do have an edge here, but it can quickly be ruined if you assume that you don't need to get her attracted to you again. I will talk about building attraction again later on in this section.

Date location

The date location isn't important for the sake of the location (it doesn't matter if you take her to a place with good coffee, or great coffee, although a great place is better then just a good one...), you will be using the location of the date to demonstrate qualities that make you more attractive.

First, never ask her to pick a location, or ask her what kind of things she likes. Not that you don't care, but right now, you are demonstrating your leadership and ability to make decisions by picking a place and telling her that that's where you are going to meet.

I consider myself a kind and considerate person, but for a first date, I'll make a girl drive half way cross town if I have to so she can see that I have these qualities. You'd be surprised how many girls would actually agree to drive half way cross town just to meet with a guy who displays strong leadership and decision making qualities.

Second, don't set yourself up for a long and tedious date. Imagine that you have to spend a 5 course dinner in a fancy restaurant with someone who turns out to be boring or unattractive to you, or if you've planned an elaborate evening of activities and then find out the girl isn't what you are looking for. Also, think about it from her perspective, the more you ask her to commit to, the less likely she is to do it so early in your relationship (she will most likely commit to meeting for a quick cup of coffee that she can eject from if she doesn't like you vs. committing to a long dinner that she will feel very uncomfortable running from early on). Of course, the short commitment can turn into a very long one once she gets to know you better, but at this point, let her believe she can easily end the date if she's not interested (on this note, **NEVER** tell her something like "you don't have to stay if you don't like me" or "you can always leave early if you're not having fun" remember – you are the reward in this interaction and she will have to be interesting enough for you to stay with her... the choice of the location is implying what the date will be like. E.g. "let's meet at the coffee shop down the street" vs. "let's meet at the airport, pack for cold weather and bring your passport"... ;).

Third, don't pick an obvious (and thus boring) location for a date. Starbucks coffee is fine for getting coffee on your way to work, but it's not the ideal location for a first time meet. Most cities have enough unique, or interesting coffee shops/bars/ etc. that allow you to show her you are not just another "cookie cutter" guy, and that you know the cool hidden places. I found this really cool yet hidden coffee shop/bar in my city and I've always gotten girls to comment on the great selection I made.

Fourth, do something you like. If you don't drink coffee, don't meet for coffee... if you hate alcohol, don't go meet at a bar. There are a million places you can meet for the first time, be creative:

If you live in a place that has good weather, go for a walk in the park or the beach. If you like art go to the museum (be prepared to show your knowledge of the art that is there, read up a bit on some of the pieces that you are going to see, so you can show her your "artistic" side and also not look like a tool when she starts talking about the paintings and all you have to say is "yeah, it's cool"...) you can also use this to be playful and creative, and tell her you will meet her by the X painting somewhere in the museum, if you set it up right, it could be quite an adventure for her to find you (of course as long as you know exactly where that painting is and that she has your cell number in case she gets lost...)

- Meet for coffee or a for a glass of wine at a cool wine bar
- Meet at the mall and go window shopping together
- If you have dogs, meet at the dog park

Make sure you meet in a place where you can eject quickly and gracefully if you aren't interested, and that the place is safe and public enough for the both of you to be comfortable.

Fifth, make sure you are meeting on your "turf". Go to a place you know well, and in an area you know well. This will reduce stress of finding the place, parking, worrying about where to sit, etc...

I also recommend taking this to the next level and creating a "date sequence".

The date sequence is a pre scripted date, which allows you to be in control of most elements of the date and to use them to your advantage.

A good date sequence involves the following:

Meet at location 1: This is a well known location to you, somewhere that the staff might already know you, and you have some sort of relationship with them (so they can say hi to you when you come in and exchange some friendly banter with you in front of your date).

Spend some time there (not more the 20-40 minutes) building attraction, and then bounce to location 2.

Location 2 is another date location, in walking distance from location 1. It could be another coffee shop/bar across the street, a dessert place, or even another part of location 1 if you don't have a good location 2 around.

You can repeat these bounces a few more times to create the illusion that you are going on more then one date that evening, I've known people who did 14 bounces in a date. It lasted the whole weekend including spending alone time in a motel together... if you bounce properly, this will seem very natural because you've already been out on "14 dates"... more on bouncing later on.

The sequence should also include a seating arrangement that is beneficial to you. Don't pick a place where you will constantly be disturbed/distracted by other people, like the bar at a busy location, or the table near the kitchen at a restaurant for example. I would go even further and set up the seating location so that she is facing a wall behind me so she can't even see the traffic going on behind her. I usually come a few minutes early to a date and pick out my seat. I also buy my own drink (unless she lost a bet and she's buying ;) and go sit down.

Chapter 16:
The Date - Part 2: The introduction and early part of the date

At this point, I'm already comfortable in my location, I usually have my drink and I am sitting and waiting for her. The place I pick for the 1st location has an upstairs section overlooking the entrance and I can easily spot her when she walks in. Depending on the situation, I wait for her to look lost (surprisingly, people rarely look up...) and then I call out to her or wave to her until she sees me. She will feel a bit embarrassed about this, and I usually tease her about not being able to find me. This sets the stage for the beginning of the date.

Buying drinks

Don't buy a woman a drink! (Unless you made the mistake and lost the bet you made with her in email - don't do that either... ;). At this point in the interaction, she's a stranger and she has to win you over. By buying her a drink you are basically saying that you want her attention and are willing to spend money to get it.

If you encounter a woman who really insists on you buying her a drink or has some other issues about that, and you still want to continue the date with her, make her do something for you and then you can buy her a drink. E.g. make her buy you a drink, and then it's fair, or tell her to make animal noises, or do a stupid dance for you, or make her tell you a funny joke, anything small like that that makes her feel she "worked" for the drink and is not getting it just because she's attractive.

Introductions

When you first meet, you will be tempted to shake her hand - Don't!

You are not meeting a business partner, or a new male friend, you are meeting for romantic purposes. Lean in for a hug, and kiss her on the cheek.

Some people (especially Asian cultures) are very wary of kissing or hugging people they don't know, so calibrate. If you see her body language is very closed off (head down, no smile, arms crossed etc. (for more info on body language, you can read "Body Language Secrets: A Guide During Courtship & Dating", by R. Don Steele) then just go for the handshake.

If you do use a handshake, try to make it a bit different, come in from the top, hi 5 her, give her "the rock" (close your fist and hold it out, she will close her fist and hit yours) that will still make you more unique then most guys.

It's very important to calibrate to this, if your emails were all about having fun and enjoying life and had a very upbeat theme to them, you should go with a more upbeat type introduction, the hug and kiss on the cheek, a hi 5 or something similar. If your emails were more on the serious or intellectual side, then a handshake is more appropriate.

When you do the hug, don't be a pervert and squeeze her close to you, this is just an introduction, you want her to feel comfortable with you, there will be more time to squeeze her close later on if you play your cards right...

Conversation tips for the first part of the date:
How to build attraction

You and your date will be tempted to go into the boring "interview" type questions. The reason for this is, that social programming has caused the both of you to think that asking questions like "where are you from" and "what do you do" are the best way to get to know a person and to determine their value as a potential mating partner. While getting to know the other person is a good way to determine their value, interview style questions are one of the worst and most boring methods to do so.

Think of it this way, does it really change who you are as a person - I mean your real core self, not just the superficial stuff - if you went to school in X instead of Y, or if you like X on TV and not Y? These questions are asked in order to try to find common interests and use that to establish rapport, but you don't need interview Q&A to establish attraction!

As I mentioned before, you will need to recreate the attraction she had for you when the two of you were emailing each other. How did you get her attracted in the first place? It was funny stories, teasing, creating sexual tension and being playful and fun. This is exactly the same thing you need to do to create attraction in the real world!

When a "regular" date usually starts, there's this awkward moment of silence and then start the interview questions. Don't have a regular date! be exciting, fun, and creative. Just start talking, talk about whatever, but don't get dragged into Q&A, tell her a funny thing that happened to you on the way over (and it doesn't have to be something that actually happened to you on the way over, just a funny story from your life that happened at some point and that you can tie into the conversation (for this, there are many "canned" stories that you can find online, they are really great, but at some point you will want to use your own "material" because you are more connected to it and because if you ever get into a relationship with that girl it will be very hard for you to explain where your "bungee jumping friend" from that story you told on the first date (the one you found online) vanished to...) let the conversation flow. Think of this not as a "date" but as a conversation you are having with a friend you haven't seen for a long time.

Initially, you will need to use the same type stories you told in emails. Find stories that get you excited. No one wants to be on a date with a person who is just reciting events that happened to them. If you get excited she will feel that excitement and it will get her charged up as well, this will lead to a high energy date and to what is called "chemistry".

In the first part of the date, your goal is to get the energy level up, have her laughing as much as possible, playing with her, teasing her, challenging her (remember the email games? You can do the same here too). But there is an order to things even in this early stage.

This goes back to commitment, the more commitment you want out of her (like if you want her to actively participate in a game) the more she needs to be excited and attracted to you. You should try to start with telling stories and teasing a bit. Some good teases are:

(All to be said with a smile, you're not trying to insult her, you are teasing her)
- If she has a big purse – "I see you brought your bowling ball with you" while pointing at the bag and smiling
- If she's short "you're really cute for a short girl"
- If she is very jittery and excited, call her energizer bunny and ask if she has an off switch

- If she appears tired, ask her if she forgot to have her frosted flakes this morning

Over time, you will come up with some great teases of your own, be creative and always calibrate to the situation. I've been with girls who come from different cultural backgrounds and totally missed the "tease" value of my comment.

Dealing with tests

This is a big one - women will test you. They don't do this consciously, they don't want to be mean, but it's a given fact. Surprisingly, a test from a woman is actually a good thing!

What it means is that she is attracted enough to you to want to see if you can handle her and if the personality qualities she sees in you aren't fake.

Some tests from women could be:

"So why aren't you married?", "what kind of car do you drive?", "I only date tall/rich/whatever guys", "why are you asking me this?"... And the list goes on, tests are basically anything a woman says to challenge your "authority" and to make you try to justify yourself or try to qualify yourself to her. These tests start the moment you meet her, and go until you are both in bed together. They even carry over into the relationship to some extent.

Tests are great, because once you know how to identify them, you can use them to demonstrate that you are a high value man, and they are really easy to handle...

The best way to handle a test from a woman, is simply to ignore it and move on...

Now, as a guy, you must be thinking, "what do you mean ignore it? that's just rude, she asked a question and I need to answer it". That's guy thinking, as a guy, you would feel hurt if someone just ignored your question and moved on to another subject, but it's different for girls, they don't take it so hard, because they are socially and genetically coded to follow a man's lead. If they meet a man powerful enough to lead them, they will gladly follow.

Be a leader, don't qualify yourself or justify what you said, and don't try to use logic to explain something you said or did to a woman.

Some real life examples:
Her: "you know, I don't usually hold hands with a guy so early on the date"
Me: look her in the eyes and take her hand (loser guy would try to justify holding hands or quickly back off).
Her: "it feels good"
Actions speak louder then words

Another way to deal with a test is to reply in a funny way, disarming it with humor.

Her: "So what kind of car do you drive?"
Me: "oh, I don't have a car, I have my mommy drive me around everywhere, in fact, she's sitting over there at the bar getting sloshed waiting for the date to end..." (I say this with a totally serious face, but with a hint of a smile, she doesn't know what to make of this, am I serious? or am I joking? Because this is such a unique answer, she bursts into laughter.

Accepting the comment is a powerful way to deal with a test:

Her: "you're really dressed well and you're very well groomed, are you gay?" she says this to try to get me to get defensive, and to see if I am comfortable with my sexuality.
Me: "yeah, you're right, you got me, I'm gay" then in an exaggerated "gay" voice, "I'm actually meeting you to get my boyfriend jealous, he's so FABOULOUS!"

Now she's laughing hysterically... not only am I comfortable with my sexuality, I can also make her laugh. Imagine how loser guys would behave when someone accused them of being gay (in this context it doesn't even make sense, it's just a test). They would get all defensive and say "no I'm not" or start bragging about all the women they've been with... look how easily you can make a difference in your response to a test and prove your higher value...

Body Language:

You've probably read many times about how verbal communication is just a small fraction of overall communications (voice tone and body language are the majority of what is being communicated) – if you don't believe me, try this:

Walk up to a random stranger in a relaxed way, with a smile on your face and in a confident but soft voice ask them for the time. Unless they are jerks, they will smile back and respond, and perhaps even start a short conversation with you.

Now, try this (if you do, you might get beaten up, so try this at your own risk or with someone you know well...), walk up to that person, in a fast pace, leaning forward with an angry look on your face, and in a loud voice ask for the time, I can almost guarantee that that person will be very defensive, protective and wonder if he/she did something wrong or if they are in danger... in both cases, you used the exact same words, but your physical approach and voice tone changed the subject's response to you.

Body language is an extremely important aspect of your communications. In this context, I'm not talking about what most people think of when they talk about dating body language; this section will not be about "if she strokes her hair twice and holds her palms up, then she likes you..." type body language.

Although I believe that reading body language is a good skill to have, I don't think it's as important as projecting good body language. Obviously, there are some tell tale signs that she likes you (like pressing her breasts together, flipping her hair at you etc...) but those only mean she likes you in the moment and is responding positively to you, not that you're done and she's ready to sleep with you now. (More on reading body language later on in the book).

The body language you project will add power to the words you say, and make you more attractive.

If you are sitting in a lounge, or coffee shop, be relaxed and lean back. Don't hunch over and lean on the table/bar. Keep your legs and arms uncrosses, and don't hold your drink in front of your chest if you are standing (hold it by your side). In fact, try to keep as much clear space between you and her, this shows that you are open, comfortable, and relaxed and not trying to set any barriers between the two of you.

Try to take up more space then you usually do. You can do this in many ways, e.g. at the bar, turn with your back to the bar, lean back and extend your arms to the sides so that you are "taking over" the 2 spots around you. At a coffee shop, lean back and put your arm on the chair next to you even if it's at another table and "take it over" so it is "your space" now.

When you talk to her, keep your body loose and free flowing. Don't be rigid and look like Frankenstein, women don't like that... ;).

Use your hands when you talk. Now when I say that, I don't mean that you need to start a freak show and wave your hands around like a crazy person, what I mean is don't leave your hands by your side holdings the armrests of the chair as if they are your safety net.

The more you use your body to convey your energy, the easier it will be for you to get creative and fun and talk about more interesting things. If you are stiff and rigid, then all your energy is bottled up in your head, and it is much harder to release it.

If you are walking on the date, or walking to her, walk a "centered walk". A centered walk is a term borrowed from martial arts. What you need to do in order to be centered is focus on a spot 2 inches under your bellybutton, and imagine there is a string there that is pulling your whole body forward. Feel the weight of your upper body on lean on that area. You are essentially leading your body with your pelvis.

Walking like this will give you a more sexual appearance (for those of you who still don't understand why, think about what lies just below that centering point...), it will also relax your body, and move your shoulders back so that you look bigger and more confidant.

When you walk, don't rush. Don't look like you are in a hurry or eager to get somewhere, you are just walking along, taking your time, I'll quote John Travolta in the movie "be cool" when he talks about getting somewhere in time – "if you're important enough, they'll wait for you" (or something like that, you get the point...), you want to look like you are important enough for her to want to be with you.

This will take some practice, especially the centered walk part, but if you can keep this in your mind at least part of the time, and practice it daily, it will eventually become natural to you.

Chapter 17:
The Date - Part 3: Mid date

By now you should already be at the first location of your date, and in the midst of some sort of conversation, you should be leading the conversation by telling stories, changing the subject when you feel like it, and keeping on teasing her and playing with her as the conversation continues.

Leading the conversation

I try to keep several conversation threads going at the same time - I.e. I start one story, and then before I come to the conclusion of that I start another story, and so on.

I don't usually use transition lines for this (Transition line - something that helps you logically connect between stories). Again, this is guy thinking – you are not telling the story to convey information to her. When you talk to a girl, she doesn't really care about the content of what you are saying, but about the emotions this is creating in her (e.g. the girl doesn't care about what types of fish you saw on your diving vacation, she does however, care about the sense of adventure and excitement your trip conveys).

I keep going back and forth between stories, and I've found that this is very effective in keeping her interested in what you are saying and keeping her engaged in the conversation.

Just imagine listening to 5 stories that are about 10 minutes long one after the other, or on the other hand, having a 50 minute conversation going about many different things.

You might be a very linear thinker, I know I am, so this will take some practice, but once you get this done, you will find that you are sweeping the girl into your reality, and she is hanging on your every word...

If you still feel the need to use transition lines, you can go with something like "oh, that reminds me..." or "oh, I just remembered, did you hear about...." or something similar to that, it doesn't actually have to remind you of something, and the girl will never question the actually has a logical link.

Topics of conversation:

As the date progresses, you will be able to tell what kind of person you are dealing with. Is she fun, intellectual, philosophical, conservative, adventurous etc? It will take you some time to learn this, but listen to how she talks, and watch how she reacts to what you say. Also, use what you talked about in email as conversation starters to get things going until you can figure this out.

Once you know what type of person she is, you can more easily calibrate your stories. If she is very conservative, the story of all the naughty stuff you did in Vegas won't really work in your advantage. If she's a party girl, you probably won't want to bring up your thoughts on 16th century Italian poetry at this point. Of course, people have many facets and the party girl might really like Italian poetry, but initially, you are not trying to get to know all the aspects of her life, just to determine if you and she get along.

Some girls might need some encouragement to get engaged in a conversation. A first "blind" date could be very intimidating for a girl. I've actually asked girls if they are nervous on our first date, and was surprised to find out that the hot and supposedly confidant girl was really nervous about meeting me (some girls have actually told me they lost sleep the night before we met!). If you encounter a girl who is having trouble engaging in regular conversation, either because she is nervous, or just plain uninteresting, and you still want to continue the date, try finding something she is passionate about, it helps if you can remember the profile and emails you exchanged, and the main topics she talked about.

Once you talk about her passion, she is most likely going to open up a bit more and talk about other subjects as well. Of course, sometimes things just don't work, don't take it to heart, just learn from it, deal with it and move on....

The reason I split the date into different parts is because conversation styles and topics will be very different in the early stages of the date and the middle and end part of it.

How do you know you are in the middle part of the date?

Mid date does not necessarily mean the actual time you are on a date (so if the date is 1 hour, the middle is not necessarily at the half hour point).

Mid-date is the point where you are no longer gauging each others interest and attraction to each other and you are starting to get to know the other person as a person (going from very broad conversation topics to very deep ones).

In the first part of the date, you will be teasing her, playing with her, making her laugh hysterically, and basically being fun for her. You are doing this to build attraction. At some point she will start showing indicators of interest for you. Indicators of interests (IOIs) are behaviors that indicate that she is becoming attracted to you. Some of these include:

- She touches you casually (there's no such thing as casual touching, she will be doing this unconsciously), not in an overt or sexual way of course, but like when she reaches over to get the sugar and brushes against your hand or when she walks next to you and brushes her shoulder against you
- She keeps eye contact and smiles at you when you are talking
- She presses her breasts together with her elbows as if to show them off to you (sounds crazy but girls actually do this!)
- She leans towards you when you are talking to listen in, or leans forward to show off her cleavage
- She starts asking you detailed questions about yourself (e.g. someone who is uninterested will not care where your parents are from)
- If there is a pause in conversation, she will try to fill it.
- She laughs at things you say that are not that funny
- She will follow if you lead her (like if you tell her to come with you to the bar)
- If she's still there... as long as she's still there and engaged in conversation, she is interested on some level...

One IOI is not enough, it could just be random or you could be reading too much into something that isn't really there. You should wait for at least 3 or 4 IOIs before you move to the next phase of conversation (3 or 4 in a short period of time. If your date is 3 hours long and you've only gotten 3 IOIs spread over the 3 hours then she's not attracted...).

Her turn:

The next phase is a very short one. Now that she's attracted to you (you know that by the IOIs you got), it's time to slowly shift the balance in conversation and make it more mutual.

You see, in the first part of the date, you probably did a lot of talking, you told funny stories, you played games with her, and she was laughing all along. If you keep doing this all throughout the date, she will have a good time, but would think that you are not interested in her for who she really is. How could you be interested if all you did was talk all the time (usually about yourself) and didn't ask her anything about herself?

The easiest way to transition into this segment of conversation is to ask her something like "tell me about yourself, what do think makes you special?" Ask this in a friendly tone, don't be aggressive or confrontational.

If she is attracted to you, she will gladly answer this question and feel that you are interested in getting to know her as a person as well.

On the other hand, if she doesn't answer, or says something like "I don't know" or whatever, you might want to keep going a bit more with funny stories and start of date type material and try this again a few minutes later. You could also help her out by eliciting an answer from her with guiding questions and positive responses (e.g. "what do you like to do?" she says "dance", "dance? Cool! What does dancing make you feel" then go into a conversation of what feelings she gets/what experiences she's had on the dance floor etc...)

After she's seen that you are interested in her as a person, comes the most important part of the date.

Moving to the next phase

At this point, you both feel that you like each other. She's attracted to you because you conveyed your personality well enough by telling funny stories, and she also feels that you are attracted to her because of what "makes her special".

Now you are going to tone down the teasing type behavior, and start getting deeper into her personality and the things you have in common.

I'm not saying that from this point the date becomes a boring intellectual effort, you will still keep it fun, but you won't tease her as much anymore, you won't treat her like a bratty kid, and you will see that the conversation is more balanced and slower paced.

At this point you will be asking her questions about what's really important to her in her life, about her childhood, about her favorite things and people in her life. Make sure you really get detailed about this, ask her things like "why are you best friends with this person" and get her emotions built up on positive things like "what do you feel when you are skiing down a mountain" this is also the time for you to share stories that are more on the intimate/sentimental side, things from your past (REMEMBER – always keep it positive, no talks about how your mom beat you when you were a kid...)

Bouncing:

This is also a good time for bouncing to a new location.

You'd be surprised how easy it is to bounce to a new location, you don't really need an excuse, but if you need one to make you comfortable you can use one of the following:

"Hey, I'm hungry lets go across the street for a bite to eat"

"They have this really cool _____ in this bar next door, come on, let's go"

"I need some cake, let's go to the dessert place on the corner"

Etc...

Notice that all these are not REQUESTS for her to come with you, you don't need her permission to go, you are going, and she is welcome to join, but she's not necessary...

If you want to be even more elaborate, you can steer the conversation towards the topic of bouncing/other interesting/tasty things close by and get her to think that was her idea. I've gotten girls to buy me dinner/cake/drinks etc. doing this.

Bouncing is a powerful technique because it makes the girl feel like she knows you already and you are on a 2nd or more dates. The image she will have in her mind is that you came into the place as strangers but now you are leaving together as a couple and going to do things together. You can even mini-bounce and take her to a different part of the date location you are in (like if you meet at the bar and talk for a while, say "let's grab a table and sit down"). This is not as powerful as a full bounce, but it still helps if you don't have a choice. Your ideal date location will be in an area that allows multiple bounces.

This is also the phase for playing different kind of games.
At this point, you are no longer qualifying her or trying to show her your value. Now you are trying to help her think of the two of you as a couple.

A great fun game is a future projection game where you talk about how things will be with you together in the future.

I highly discourage future projection games involving the two of you being married and having lots of babies etc... This will just freak her out and put pressure on her, but what you can do is talk about a trip you are going to take together. E.g. if she says she likes to ski, you can say something like "yeah, we should go to Colorado, it'll really be cool" and then go into all the details of the activities the ski resort has to offer and how you will do them together (don't get into any intimate talk at this point, unless she starts including it in the conversation).

Keep things fun and upbeat and just let the conversation flow while you lead it to where you want it to go.

Getting physical

I recommend getting physical from the first second you meet her.

I bet you think I'm crazy...;) what I mean by getting physical, is slowly escalating the amount of physical contact you and her have over the date.

Disclaimer: Remember – never force any physical contact on a girl or try to get physical if she says "no"!

Imagine this – you've had a fun date, and now you are at her car. You lean in for a kiss but she backs off. Why did she do that? She might have had a lot of fun with you, but she didn't have any physical contact with you whatsoever, going from nothing to a kiss feels weird...

Now, imagine that you give her a warm hug and kiss on the cheek when you meet, lightly and casually touch her hand during the date, guide her as you walk to the table by lightly placing your hand on her lower back, holding her hand (not necessarily in a romantic way at first – more on this later) and hugging her during different parts of the date. You've had so much physical contact, that a kiss is almost natural.

Kino (Kino from the word kinesthetic – meaning a sensory experience) is every kind of touch you and her have over the time you are together. It usually starts out very light and casual, don't try and grab her at the first sign of interest. Brush your hand against hers when you are reaching over for something, stand close enough to her so that your shoulders touch, touch her lightly as you talk, etc... This should be done often, but not in an obvious way... e.g. high five her when you find something the both of you like. There, you just touched her hand, and if both your fingers interlock for a few seconds, it is a good sign she is interested in you.

Once you've had some touch, start thinking of going for the next level which is hand holding.

Hand holding is the first "intimate" action you will have in your date. I'm not saying it's impossible to escalate to more physical contact without holding hands, but it's much more natural to escalate once you've had it.

There are several ways to lead into hand holding:

1. You could just take her hand and hold it. This is the most direct method, so this needs to be done when you feel that you have generated enough attraction and she will feel comfortable with you holding her hand. This is something you will "know" once you've been with enough women. There are no real signs or fool proof indicators that you are there, it's more a trial and error thing. You take her hand, and she resists? Then you're not there yet... if she holds your hand, you are there...

When I say "take her hand" I don't mean "grab her hand even if she is holding a drink and force her to hold your hand". I mean that you should do it in a gentle way, very casual, don't stare at her hand and look for her reactions when you are doing this, just take her hand as if it's the most natural thing to do. Don't make a big deal of it.

Remember – what isn't a big deal to you – won't be a big deal to her in most cases.

2. If you feel uncomfortable with the direct method, and you want a more subtle way to get to hand holding, then you can always try palmistry.

Palmistry (palm reading) is a great way to hold hands and initiate physical contact, and to generate conversation that shows how deep and insightful you are.

If you want to take it seriously, then there are some great books and resources online for palmistry, I personally used "Palm Reading: A Little Guide to Life's Secrets (Miniature Edition) (Hardcover) by Dennis Fairchild", it's a great little book that has lots of info on palmistry.

You don't need to actually learn how to read palms, you can just get a general idea of the main and minor lines and what they mean, and make stuff up.

Be sure to generalize enough so that you sound profound and serious and so that she can relate to it. E.g. say something like "you have a very strong heart line, it seems like you make many decisions in your life using emotions as a guide" – this is true for pretty much every person in the world, but in the context of your date, you are reading HER palm and this will resonate as true about her.

You could also use palm reading to make fun of her, joke around, and make crazy stuff up about her to make her laugh.

3. if you don't feel that palmistry is congruent with your personality, or if you feel like the vibe is not right for that (e.g. if it's a very high energy date, palmistry will ruin the energy by taking things

to a more serious and low energy level unless you incorporate it in a high energy game), you can always comment on anything on her hands and take it for a "closer look". E.g. say – "that's a cool ring/bracelet" and take her hand for a closer look. That will also give you points for noticing small things about her and make her feel good about herself for wearing them.

4. If she's not wearing any rings or bracelets and there is nothing to comment on, you can always talk about her nails and take them in for a closer look. Most girls have their nails done (or at least presentable) for a first date so that you can comment on them.

Any of these methods are good for hand holding. When you try them, make sure your hands are not sweaty or clammy, and that your nails are at least mildly presentable. She will have a closer look at your hands when you do this and if she missed your bad grooming before, she will definitely notice it now...

When you hold her hand, don't turn it into an evening long event. Hold her hand enough for her to feel good and comfortable about it, and then put it down and let go. This is also something that you will need to calibrate to, but a minute or so is usually a good start.

Once you've passed this step, holding hands again will be more natural and you should do it every now and then during your conversation (especially to reward "good behavior" from her).

You can also use the seating arrangement to your advantage for this. What I usually do is start in the first location when we are sitting facing each other like the typical date, and then when we move to the 2nd location, I make sure to sit at a table for 4 people so I can sit next to her. This creates a general sensation of "we were at the 1st location as strangers, but we got to know each other and now we are getting close both emotionally and physically", this also makes it very easy to escalate physical touch since you are very close to her.

Other physical touch escalations include putting your arm around her in a "buddy" way (around the back of her neck), stroking her hair, stroking her face, whispering in her ear (this is actually a very good one, make sure your breath is clean and fresh, and use this as a way to both stand very close to her, lean in and have larger areas of your bodies touching, holding her neck and face, and breathing in her ear, this is very powerful and should be used at least once during a date, you can just say "hey, I have a secret to tell you, come here (make her lean in to you)", then just say something funny, or even say "never mind" and smile...

Important note about physical escalation: in no point during the date, should you force physical escalation on the girl. If she indicates either verbally or with closed body language, that she is uncomfortable, then back off!!!

Saying this doesn't mean you should end the date and go home. If she is resistant to physical escalation, you can try to build more attraction by being funny and charming, and then try again later on.

Don't try to "convince" her to accept you. e.g. don't say "come on baby, let me hold your hand", NEVER try to logically convince a girl to do this, it is something that is triggered by her emotions not by logic. "Change her mood, nor her mind"...

If you see that she keeps resisting you, even though you are being funny and charming and doing all the right things, then perhaps you need to back off and take a look at what you are doing to see if you are calibrated to the situation (being loud and talking about partying in a yoga class is an example of bad calibration...) she might just be uncomfortable with public displays of affection and you need to wait till you are in a more secluded area to escalate properly.

Once you've started escalating physically, and it seems to be working (i.e. not getting resistance and she is cooperating with your escalation and looking like she's having a good time), then it is time to move to the next step.

Chapter 18:
The Date - Part 4: Ending the date: The kiss and future plans

At this point, you should both be having fun and establishing an emotional connection. You should be discussing favorite common things, childhood experiences, family etc… when I say emotional connection, I don't mean that you should be using her as a sounding board for your emotional problems or needs, nor should you be discussing how much you want to have kids and how many does she want, the whole conversation should be kept at very "light" level but still cover meaningful topics. E.g. what growing up with 2 sisters was like, favorite arts and what they make you feel, a memorable moment on a special vacation etc… make her feel like she knows you very well already, even though you've only spent a short amount of time together.

You might have the urge to keep your date going until it dies down on its own. I mean you are having fun, she is too, and you are bonding and such… right? Wrong!

If you wait till the date dies down, then you will be ending the date on a low point, and her memory of you will be of "the guy who I hit it off with at first but ended up being boring".

When you feel that you are both really having fun, and you are a very high point in the date (obviously, you should give yourself some time and not have a 20 minute date), you say something like "hey, I'm really enjoying myself, but I need to get going" and give a reason of your choosing. You could say, "I have to get up early tomorrow", "I really need to let the dogs out for a walk", "I'm waiting for a call from overseas" whatever you can come up with that makes sense and is not too lame ("I need to wash my hair" – lame…;) you could also use humor here and say something like, "ok, we need to end this, my next date *(or my 10 o'clock)* is coming soon and it would be kinda awkward for the both of you to meet" say it with a big smile and exaggerate it a bit so she knows you are kidding...

She will most likely be stunned by this, you were both having a good time, what did she do wrong? But that's good, that will increase her attraction to you. I actually learned this from a girl, we were having a great time on the date, and then she abruptly ended it. I was stumped to what went wrong, and couldn't figure it out. I obviously called her very soon after and wanted to see her again...

This works the same way for women, if you are the one who is in control, they will want to be with you. I even used to set an alarm on my cell phone that would vibrate after a certain time has passed so I know that I need to start thinking of ending the date.

Walk out of the place you are in, hold the door for her as you walk out and offer to walk her to her car/home. If she says no, then politely insist a bit, she will usually agree, she's just trying to be polite. If you are in a city where public transportation is more prominent then you might have to work around this a bit and get to the same situations as described below.

The kiss:

This is one of two most critical points in a establishing a relationship with a woman. The first is actually approaching her, which you've already done. This is the second decision point where you get to see how interested you both are in each other and where you make your intentions for her crystal clear.

You should now be at her car/door or at the point where you are both parting ways. On a side note, my approach towards online dating was to find a special woman and spend time with her in a long term relationship. Every date was a part of a longer process of getting to know the girl, I wasn't in a hurry to get her in bed, so I usually do this part after a second date, I prefer to do it that way because it gives me a chance to step back and think about the girl I met and if I want to see her again, but I've also done this at the end of first dates and was equally successful. Ok, I've been keeping you in suspense for too long... ;) the kiss...

You will be standing at her door/car, now notice her body language.

Do you remember the movie "Hitch"? There is a scene in the movie where he teaches the guy how to kiss a girl and he tells him to watch for the pause (If you didn't, I recommend you watch it, there are some good ideas in that movie even though I think the underlying concept is wrong but that's a different discussion...). The pause I'm talking about is this – if you want to just drive away in your car, you would just open the door, get in and drive right? But if there is a "kiss window", where the girl is hoping to get kissed, she will pause, even for a slight moment before she gets in the car. You should be looking for that pause.

At this point I usually do the following:

First, I move into "her space". This is the personal space around her that would not be invaded during normal day to day interactions (again, I say, "move into her space" not "get in her face" this should all be done very slowly and very calmly).

Since there is a pause, I take my hand and slightly touch her hair, and brush it away from her face. If you've physically escalated properly, this shouldn't be an issue, and if it is (she flinches or you get a negative vibe) then you probably need to escalate a bit more or build more attraction before you go for the kiss.

I then say something like "your hair is really beautiful/soft/nice" and slowly caress it while very lightly touching her cheek with the tips of my fingers.

She should be getting chills from this and in some cases you can actually see her getting excited by this. I then move from caressing her hair to caressing her face. If all goes well with this, then I move in for a kiss.

How to kiss?

Every person has a unique kissing style, I like the 2 step approach and it's worked well for me. The key to this again is to build anticipation and make her feel like she wants more.

When you first kiss her, get close to her very slowly, and very lightly touch her lips with yours. When I say lightly, I mean VERY lightly. The second you feel even the slightest contact with her, slowly move away, and better yet, slowly push her away – I'll explain why later on. This will put her into emotional turmoil again. Most guys she's ever kissed (if not all of them) would try to take as much as they can out of this situation and try to kiss her more, French her, or whatever. She will again wonder if something is wrong, if she's a bad kisser, she has bad breath, you don't like her, etc...

This all take place in her head in an instance and builds enormous attraction since women are genetically and socially inclined to be people pleasers.

At this point, while you are still close to each other, I look in her eyes, smile and go in again, this time for a longer kiss.

It's important to note here, that you shouldn't be trying to escalate the kiss into anything else at this point. No tongue, no feeling of intimate body parts, no squeezing her against you, nothing like that, just lips. Kiss for about 5 seconds, and then push her away very lightly but in a way that she feels you pushing her.

This is another one of those counter intuitive things that work wonders. If you push her away, you will be separating yourself from all the other guys who want to cling to her and be with her. She won't be able to figure this out because most guys don't push her away while kissing. This type of behavior triggers a deep attraction mechanism in her that she cannot control.

If she tries to escalate the kiss, or if she protests about you pushing her away, this is even better! This is where you say something like "slow down, I don't know you well enough yet". You are switching the frame of the interaction on her. She is used to the guys being the horny aggressive ones who always want more and now she is the one who is behaving like this. There were times where I've seen girls start behaving like loser guys and trying to kiss me again, or start calling me 10 times a day starting right after the date... just by doing this, you turn the tables on her and show her you are in control and you will be the one deciding how the physical escalation will progress. This also sets the stage for later physical interactions where she will already be used to simply following your lead.

This is the type of behavior you should exhibit by the way, all through the interaction until you get to a sexual relationship, you should always give her some sort of physical pleasure (kissing, making out etc.) and then take it away while she is enjoying herself. This will drive her nuts and make you super attractive to her. There will be time to escalate later...

What if you're not sure about kissing?

If you feel that there might have been a pause, but you aren't sure if you should go for the kiss or not, I would err on the side of **action**. Remember, you are learning a new skill and you need to be detached from the results of your action in order to make progress. The girl might be really amazing, but if you decide not to kiss her, even though she "gave" you the window, then your chances with her go down significantly...

Worst case, she'll turn her cheek to you, or say "not yet". I've even had a girl let out a "yikes" and flinch back. Oh well, I had to wait for date 3 where she ended up naked in my bed...

Some miscellaneous kissing tips:

When you are walking her to her car, walk her; don't offer to drive her there even if it's a bit far. It's much easier to create a pause and to move in for a kiss if you don't have the logistics problem of seatbelts, moving sideways, and the arm rest in between you.
Again, don't force yourself on her, step back and give her space, you can always try again some other time if she's not ready yet.

Some girls have trouble kissing or showing physical affection in public. If you feel that that is the case, make sure you try to kiss her when the area you are in is secluded. E.g. if you both park in the parking lot of a ball park and walk back after a game, then you will most likely not be able to kiss her if she is uncomfortable with all the people around.

Kissing mess ups: sometimes your coordination will not be 100% accurate and your kiss will be less then perfect (she leans in for a hug, you go for a kiss, or you bump noses or something like that), it happens, and there is no need to be un-cool about it and freak out. The best way to recover (and the most pleasurable one too) is to calmly and with a smile say something like "that's not right for our first kiss. Let's try this again" and kiss her again. I've had this happen several times and the following kisses were amazing.

If the vibe of your date is right, you can also tease her and say something like "that was about a 6... I know you can do better then that!" you will most likely get a slap on your arm and then a real good kiss...

The next step is to get her to a location where you both are in private.

You should make sure that you have a location like that ready. You should also have an "excuse" to get her there. I've always used "wanna come over and see my dogs?" because they usually come up in conversation, or the art I have in my house or whatever comes to mind, just make sure it's relevant to her as well, so unless you are both die hard trekkies don't try the "do you want to come over and see my star trek action figure collection?"

If she agrees, either give her a ride in your car, or tell her to follow you. As you are entering the car you can also say "don't get your hopes up, you're not having sex tonight" (or if you don't feel this will go well with her, you can tone it down and say "you can only come over for a few minutes/a short time"). This is another line I stole from a girl, it works wonders.

You see, sexual tension works like this – there is always a resistor and a pursuer. One of you has to play each role. I think it's much easier to get laid if the girl is the pursuer and is trying to get you to sleep with her rather then you having to get her to agree... this concept is a bit counter intuitive, but if you actively resist her by pushing her away after making an advance, and telling her things like "I need to get to know you better" or "lets slow this down" while you are getting physical, you will make amazing progress. (See my special Sexual Escalation Handbook that you get when you buy this book for more on this). Saying "you can only come over for a few minutes" makes her feel two things. First, that she is not going to have to fight you off once you get to your place, since you already created the illusion that you aren't going to do anything. And second, she is again wondering what's going on since every single guy she's ever met has always wanted to have sex with her or get her to come home with him to spend the night...

Once you get her to your place, follow the steps in the sexual escalation handbook...

Ending the date:

This part is up to you. If you are into one night stands, and would prefer to never see this girl again, then by all means, don't delude her into thinking you are going to be her boyfriend. Sometime it's even better to tell the girl up front that you are not looking for a long term relationship or to get married even if you are because that takes a lot of pressure off of her. If you are interested in meeting the girl again (for whatever reason), don't talk about a second date while you are on the first.

Make it even more ambiguous for her and have her guessing about your future intentions. At some point in the date, if the girl likes you, she'll start hinting towards meeting again by saying stuff like "yeah, we should definitely do that next time" when you talk about an activity you want to do, or she might hint towards future activities that are happening in town so you can ask her out to them.

This is great because you can confuse her even further and increase her need to chase after you by saying (if she talks about "next time") "well, sure, if I want a next time", or if she drops future events just smile and move on to a different subject. This will really keep her guessing about your intentions and why you are not like all other guys she's ever been out with that would start planning their future together on a first date... this of course, builds her attraction to you even further.

I've even gone as far as having a girl ask me if I want her phone number (remember – I never call girls) and me saying, "why would I want that?" and giving her a sly smile...

After ending the date and parting ways, you should wait 1 to 3 days, and then re-initiate contact. **NEVER** call/email/text her right after the date! That is super needy and clingy and will make her run like crazy! If you feel that you must contact her NOW because she is so special and you can't wait to tell her all the thoughts that are on your mind, write an email, **DON'T** send it, and save it as a draft. That should get some of your anxiousness out of the way while not compromising the attraction you built for her.

One more thing you should **NEVER EVER** do is ask for feedback or validation **during or after** the date. What I mean is asking something like "so how am I doing?". The message that this sends is that you are a needy man who is looking for validation from a woman, and not only are you incapable of figuring out how you are doing on the date (a sign that you haven't had much experience with women, hence you must not have value to women), but you also need a woman to validate your behavior (leaders don't look to others for validation, they know that what they are doing is the right thing).

A 2nd date follow up I usually use is something like this:

Template 5: 2nd date email
Hey (her name)
I had fun with you the other night; you seem like a cool person. I was just thinking of (insert something especially funny or witty or stupid she did) *and I cracked a smile, you get 5 points for that...*
Lets meet up again sometime, I'm busy on (pick random day) *but I'm free on* (another day) *there's this really great restaurant/ pub/ beach/ event that I'm sure you'll like.*
Talk to you soon,
(Your name)

Again, keep your online/phone contact to a minimum and let her look forward to another great date with you. If you have sex with a girl on the first date, you would probably be better off giving her a call if you want to see her again, but use a similar format for the phone conversation.

Phone game:

Phone calls at this point shouldn't be very long, a few minutes max. You should start by telling her that you only have a few minutes to talk (to show you aren't too available to her yet), and say pretty much the same thing as in the template above. You could also tell her a funny story about something that happened to you that day, or just something to remind her about her attraction to you.

If she doesn't answer and you get her voice mail, don't hang up, or leave a 10 minute message! What you do is tell her that you called, and you will try again later that day around a certain hour. E.g. "hey Lisa, it's Sam, I'll try to call you again around 9pm. Talk to you soon". This way, she doesn't have the pressure of calling you back (girls don't usually call guys), and you don't need to play phone tag. If she's interested, she will be available at 9, and if she really can't make it, she will let you know some how. There is also the option that she just didn't get your message in time, which can happen, so follow up a couple of days later.

One last tip: you might be tempted to spend a lot of time with a specific girl early on because she is fun/beautiful or whatever. Make sure that you don't spend more then one to two days a week max with a girl unless you want her to be your girlfriend. Any more then that then she will either feel that you are too available and lose attraction, or she will develop feelings for you and then you will really hurt her when she finds out your true intentions for her.

Chapter 19: Epilogue

Over the last few years, I've made some amazing personal transformations.

I started out being a loser guy, who didn't get much attention from girls online or offline, but over time, I became a "ladies man". This has gotten to a point where my married neighbor lives vicariously through me and keeps a tab of the girls that spend the night at my place (he already gave up on trying to remember their names if they happen to bump into him on their way out...).

I've gone from a guy who had no women in his life, to a guy that is literally forced to choose between 4 beautiful, sexy, intelligent, young women and break the hearts of 3 of them by turning them down (I've also dated multiple women at the same time, I just don't have the time or the energy to deal with the logistics of this... ;).

Most of all, I've developed as a person. I used to be a guy who got his validation and sense of self worth from women. If a woman would give me the time of day, I'd be so happy and if woman shot me down I was devastated. I felt that high quality women are really rare, out of my league and if I found one, I needed to hold on to her and give her anything she wanted so she'd be with me. This is not the reality I live in now.

I know that there is an abundance of available, attractive women out there.

I am deeply in love with my girlfriend, I am loyal to her and I would feel pain if she left me, but I know that if that ever happens, I can get another 20 dates, and have 4 beautiful women begging for my attention and affection (both physical and emotional) within a couple of weeks.

I no longer need women to validate my worth, and that makes me even more attractive to them. This has also made me more confident in other aspects of life, and my career, social circle, and overall happiness are much greater then they were at any other point in my life.

If you follow the instructions in this book and keep doing so until you get good at this, your success with women will skyrocket and you will experience things that you've never believed possible.

Good luck!!!
Sam Stone

Appendix A:
The importance of friendship with women

I want to talk about friendship with women, which is something I feel that I have to include in this book even though it doesn't tie directly to online dating.

Most guys have gotten the "lets just be friends" line from a woman before, and that's fine, if she doesn't want to be in a relationship with you, it's her loss, since you are the reward. But you have to differentiate that from when a woman says "let's be friends"!

You see, even though the wording might be similar, when a woman wants to be "just" friends, it usually translates into "I would really be ok with not ever seeing or hearing from you again", BUT, most high quality women are capable of being friends with guys in a non sexual way.

This usually requires a mental switch to go off in a guy's head. You see, as a man, you are genetically programmed to want to have sex with a woman. Most guys who are "friends" with a girl are actually orbiting around her and hoping to "friend" her into having sex with them in a moment of weakness. If you are capable of developing the ability to befriend a woman without the need to have sex with her (and I highly recommend that you develop that ability) you will discover that friendships with women can lead to some very valuable rewards.

I've met some really amazing women online, some of them became romantic partners, and some didn't. I've tried to stay friend with several of the special women I met online who I think could make good friends and have things to offer in my life.

I've spent time with these women, learning more about them and how women think, getting fashion advice and expanding my social status and circle of friends (there were times when I walked into a bar with 2 hot women (both friends) and had every single woman in the place check me out.

Most guys would get pissed off if a woman told them she wants to be their friend, and act like little babies who didn't get their way. But maintaining friendship with women is a great way to gain insight into a world you don't usually have access to. Besides, most hot women have hot friends...

Appendix B:
Your personal "Video game" success plan:

The levels of the "video game" are the steps in the APL-IED method:

- **Pre game Level 1** – figure out who you are and what you want, this happens before you even turn on the computer.
- **Pre game Level 2** – get your profile together. This is the preparation part of the game, this is like the tutorial level some games have, that will help you set up for later in the game.
- **Game Level 1** – the search - you are hunting for a target.
- **Game Level 2** – this is where you get in the game and start playing – you will use the tools you put together in the pre game levels to write a good first email that gets consistent responses. Wining the level – once you get over a 30% response rate to your first email (more then 30% of the girls you email respond positively ("get away from me freak" does not count in this... ;)
- **Game level 3** – to win this level you will need to get into a dialogue with girls who responded to you. Your secret weapon in this level is the **Sam Stone™ email method**.
- **Game level 4** – to win this level, you will need to get the girl to go on a date with you. You will use the **Sam Stone™ email method** and the things you learned in previous levels to win this.
- **Game level 5** – to win this level, you will need to have a successful 1st date. The **Sam Stone™ date method** will be your weapon of choice here.
- **Game level 6** – the bonus round – winning this level depends on your goals, whether you want lots of one night stands, or to meet a special girl to be in a relationship with, this is where it all happens.

www.ingramcontent.com/pod-product-compliance
Lightning Source LLC
Chambersburg PA
CBHW022152080426
42734CB00006B/400